THE
HACHLAND HILL
COOKBOOK

THE RECIPES & LEGACY *of* PHILA HACH

THE
HACHLAND HILL
COOKBOOK

THE RECIPES & LEGACY *of* PHILA HACH

CARTER HACH

Foreword by
LISA DONOVAN

BLUE
HILLS
PRESS

Publisher: Matthew Teague
Editor: Erin Byers Murray
Design: Lindsay Hess
Assistant Publisher: Josh Nava
Photography: Danielle Atkins
Index: Jay Kreider

Blue Hills Press
P.O. Box 239
Whites Creek, TN 37189

hardback: 978-1-951217-45-7
eBook ISBN: 978-1-951217-39-6
Library of Congress Control Number: 2022940699
Printed in the United States
10 9 8 7 6 5 4 3 2 1

Note: The following list contains names used in *The Hachland Hill
Cookbook* that may be registered with the United States Copyright
Office: ABC; American Airlines; Angel's Envy; Angostura; Birddog
Whiskey; Coca-Cola; Cracker Barrel; Crisco; Culinary Institute of
America; Dubonnet; Duke's; Ford's London Gin; French Culinary
Institute; Fresh Market; Funyon; Huy Fong Foods; Instant Pot; Jack
Daniels; KFC; Knorr; Kroger; Lowry's; Lustau; Maggi; Natural Light;
Old Port; Opryland; Pillsbury; Plantation Barbados Rum; Plaza Hotel;
Pommery; Prego; Prichard's; Purity; Pyrex; Reese's; Sauce Arturo;
Sprite; Tabasco; Vermont Creamery; Wood River Creamery; Woodford
Reserve; WSM; Ziploc

To learn more about Blue Hills Press books, or to find a retailer near you,
email info@bluehillspress.com or visit us at www.bluehillspress.com.

DEDICATION

I'd like to dedicate the book to Phila and my daughter, her granddaughter, Lane Olivia Hach, and to all of the grandmothers who pass along recipes as well as a passion for cooking to our youth.

CONTENTS

RECIPE DIRECTORY

Chapter 3:
MEATS & ACCOMPANIMENTS

RECIPE DIRECTORY

[CONTINUED]

Chapter 6:
LARDER

Lisa Donovan

FOREWORD

THERE IS AN UNDENIABLE THING, with a capital T, that happens when you spend any amount of time baking—but, it seems, most especially when you spend a professional amount of time baking. Baking can shake loose the isolation of hard times. Baking can bring you strange clarity and connectivity. Baking often brings you back to something very basic, nearly primal, about being human. And in all of those things, it brings that undeniable Thing that you realize you gained without so much as even trying: a tether to other humans, in the past and in the present alike, who have made those same moves, who have taken and continue to take their shelter in a bin of flour, who have worked their hands into a bowl of sugar to rub lemon zest or vanilla bean seeds into the grains of cane to bring out a scent, a flavor, a beginning to something more complete. That Thing begins to feel like a space you've entered, a crowded room full of history and meaning, and a potential pathway to some kind of understanding about where you (and others) are and have been. You might just feel, all of a sudden, like a member of a collective, if you want to look at it that way—a sensational club of people who need their hands to be finding meaning in the tradition of baking, cooking, hospitality, and generosity. That Thing is broader than kinship and more intimate than community. But it is simple in its basic appeal: just a mere ethereal recognition of who we all are that can open you right up and out.

This was how I first found Phila Hach, not as a real human in front of me but as a permeation in the Nashville air. Without even knowing her name, she was involved in an unsinkable and unshakable feeling I started to get while I was beginning my work in a kitchen that baking was bringing me closer to the right things, the right future, and, most importantly, the right people. And, true to my instinct, when I first met Phila I simply thought, "well there she is!" as if I knew her already, because I felt I did—simply from the years I spent with my hands doing the same work hers did.

It's commonly said that food brings people together and, while I now have muddled feelings about the complications imbued in a statement like this, food certainly brought me to Phila. And, upon reading this incredible book, it can be easily said that food brought Phila to the world. You will find within these pages that Phila Hach was not a simple character but rather a remarkably powerful woman who changed the scope of so many cultural expectations through her work and grit and refreshing worldview. I'd imagine that like most women of her time, people easily attempted to see her in a way that reduced her to "simply a woman who could cook a thing or two." It has always been easy to assume that women who make careers in food lack a certain skill—after all, isn't a woman's place in the kitchen? Why embellish it with any true value? Phila transcended those mediations of this work and insisted upon a kind of respect for all who engage in it. And, not for nothing, she did so with wit, style, a wicked sense of humor and, above all, an immense dedication and love to and for her craft and fellow cooks.

In my dining room hangs a large photograph of Phila's hands making biscuits. I look at it every day and every day it reminds me of what baking means and why I am so fortunate to count myself amongst others in this work. It also reminds me that Phila Hach is still, and will always be, a part of the never-ending story that is written in the simple task of pouring some buttermilk into some flour to feed a friend or a stranger. This book, so beautifully written by her torch-bearing grandson, is a beautiful pathway to that Thing we all seek, that celebration of life and of each other and of the understanding that we all come from something so basic and good. It is, mostly, a beautiful glimpse into one of the finest women to ever embody this celebration entirely.

Phila Hach at the Tobacco Barn, Hachland Hill, 2014

Carter Hach

INTRODUCTION

I WAS IN MY GRANDMOTHER'S KITCHEN from the beginning. Chocolate nut drop cookies were the first recipe I made with "Phifee," which is what my brother, sister, and I called Phila Hach when we were growing up. In my barely legible handwriting, on the front page of one of her cookbooks, I wrote the recipe's title clearly before I was even old enough to spell the words correctly. Years later, in 2001, Phila found the note and transcribed her own message on the page. "To Hachland Hill's next Chef." Phila never gave it to me herself, but a former employee unearthed the book while looking for my grandmother's fudge pie recipe and returned it to me in 2017. Little did Phila know that her prediction would come true.

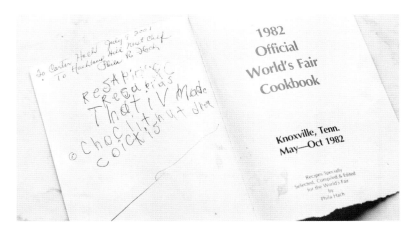

The woods around Joelton long beckoned Phila Hach. "No matter where you roam in this world, there will always be something about those woods and going up that little creek, bedrock thousands of years old, squishing my toes between all the mosses," she once told me. "Unless the world comes to an end and the spring dries up, which it's not, those woods are home."

I can remember her, hand-in-hand, leading us children up that slick creek bed. Once we got to the spring, climbing the rocks against the current, my siblings and I would carry on, splashing about, turning up stones in search of crawdads and arrowheads. I can still feel all those mosses squishing between our toes, and there is still something about those woods. Bent trees make a tunnel over the creek, and as I gaze out over it, as far as my eyes allow, I can see out past the 150-year-old tobacco barn, the water surface shimmering with the colors of fall foliage. The world hasn't come to an end, and the spring is still as wet as when God spilled the first drops of water in its hole. Those woods, Hachland Hill, and its kitchen are home to me, as they always were to Phila. And they're as timeless as the recipes she has passed down.

After attending high school at Montgomery Bell Academy in Nashville, I studied journalism and public relations at the University of Mississippi where I also minored in English and Spanish—I've always had a love for creative writing and the art of storytelling, which to me transcends cultures and language barriers. In 2015, through the University of Virginia, I had the opportunity to study creative writing while traveling during a Semester at Sea, visiting more than 15 countries throughout Asia, South Asia, and Africa. At the same time as I was applying, Phila was diagnosed with cancer. The apprehension of knowing that my grandmother's liver was ill and her colon was corroded weighed heavy on my mind.

Staring at a blank space to determine my future, I wrestled with a decision to go on the journey or stay home. I worried she wouldn't be there when I returned. I wondered if the trip would be cut short by a call from home. I drove up from Ole Miss to visit her, sharing stories from school and filling her in on the prospect of this trip and my concerns, to which she responded: "What're you waiting for?" Phila wanted me to have my own adventures around the world like she had during her days with American Airlines over half a century before.

In a split-second of scribble scrabble, I signed the papers and enrolled in the program, which did take me far from my home childhood home and worlds apart from my peers at Ole Miss and oceans away from Phila and Hachland Hill. It was hard to leave, but now I can say that I would only have regretted if I had not gone.

I was introduced to many different dishes during my time abroad, almost always taking notes, which I later used to develop my own recipes

Hachland Hill then (1978) and now (2022)

once I got back home—it was my way of marrying Southern comfort food with the many other cultural influences I'd connected with. Both the trip abroad and my time at Ole Miss eventually played significant roles in developing my palate, as both a chef and an author.

Meanwhile, the Southern Foodways Alliance, which is headquartered on campus in Oxford, inspired me to research the history of food and its deeper works. Throughout my college career, I had articles published in the Daily Mississippian, the Oxford Eagle, SFA's Magazine Gravy, the Jackson Sun, Take Em' Magazine, and many more related to food and land conservation.

On my list of priorities upon leaving Ole Miss was to pursue an MFA in creative writing—it was not to take the wheel at Hachland Hill. My brother was working full swing in real estate in New York City, and my sister would eventually plant her feet in Salt Lake City. In Phila's last year, when I visited her in hospice, a lot of our conversations turned to the future of Hachland Hill. My parents and I spoke about this on the phone often toward the end of my time at college.

My father, whose focus is on real estate in Nashville, blessed us children with so many opportunities and privileges throughout our young lives. He was about to present me with my biggest opportunity yet. Without someone stepping up to run Hachland Hill fulltime, he reluctantly announced, the property would have to be sold. It was, and is, too big of a property to simply hold onto without generating money through a functioning business. He wanted to preserve his parents' legacy, he wanted to see it succeed. I couldn't, and wouldn't, watch it go away. I became the proprietor and director of sales for Hachland Hill in May of 2016, facilitating my first wedding there as the man in charge only two weeks after graduating from Ole Miss. The business' revenue tripled in my first two years at the helm. In no time, I found myself drawn to the back of house. I would absolutely consider myself a salesman and people person, but I could not stay away from the kitchen.

This book was written to tell and preserve Phila's history as a pioneering woman in the culinary arts.

I stepped away from Hachland Hill for a quick stint in New York where I completed an intensive study of bread and pastry under chef Christopher Ciresi (formerly the executive pastry chef at Manhattan's legendary Plaza Hotel) at the French Culinary Institute (then the ICC), where I also worked on cakes under the tutelage of chefs Jürgen David and Kierin Baldwin.

Meanwhile, I also continued to learn the staples of Southern cooking from longtime Hachland Hill employee Ruth Williams, who started cooking with Phila at the age of sixteen years old and retired one year after I took over. She was like a second grandmother at Hachland Hill, and she taught me so much in her last year before handing over the rolling pin to the iconic dining inn that she helped build.

In Nashville, eager to continue learning and shaping my techniques to create unique dining experience at Hachland Hill, I staged at several notable restaurants in my nonexistent free time. I just wanted to be better. I wanted to be the best that I could for Hachland Hill, and for Phila.

I did have another opportunity—I was accepted into a masters in food business program at the Culinary Institute of America—that I had to pass by because I was too busy running Hachland Hill. I know that there is a surplus of knowledge that I passed up by making that decision, but I chose to carry the torch left for me by Phila and Ruth.

I started writing this book seven years ago. Phila's chronological tale, my upbringing in the kitchen, and all of the associated stories, were the precursor to a fictional novel that followed a young man coming to grips with the cultural differences between the American South and other regions, specifically South Asia and Africa. The fictional portion was inspired by my experiences traveling abroad. A compilation of our recipes was the proposed third part. "Family, Fiction, Food" was the title and concept in my young and eager mind.

My solicitation of the three-part literary project was steadfast, and I met rejection from almost every publishing house that I thought was worth a damn. With input from other writing professionals who have my utmost respect, including my editor, Erin Byers Murray, I came to understand that Phila's story coupled with my own could be a book of its own. What you'll find here are many of our shared stories, ones I collected through many interviews with Phila, as well as our close family members, friends, and colleagues. Of course, the recipes throughout come from us both and are meant to be a joy for anyone cooking along at home in the kitchen!

This book was written to tell and preserve Phila's history as a pioneering woman in the culinary arts and to share how she and other special people like Ruth Williams shaped me and Hachland Hill into what we are today.

I still put in 120 hours some weeks, always on my feet, working away from my wife and our dogs. The burns, sleepless nights, and so many missed occasions—I think about what Miss Ruth thought to herself as a teenager more than 60 years ago, that this lifestyle wasn't going to work.

But now, I remind myself that it was what I needed to do. It brought me full circle to those woods and to what beckons, just as it did for Phila. And the result is a beautiful thing, time and time again.

Carter Hach

A Timeline of
PHILA'S LIFE

1926	Phila's birthyear
1939	Spends one of her teenage summers at Lookout Mountain Hotel in Chattanooga, TN
1945-49	School; international stewardess; courtship with Adolf
1949	She receives her music degree (Ward-Belmont College) and a BA in Foods and Nutrition (Peabody College)
1949	Phila authors first catering manual for airline industry (written at Prince George Hotel in NYC)
1950-56	Television: *Kitchen Kollege*
1954	Publishes *Kitchen Kollege Recipes*
1956	Marriage; opening of Hachland Hill in Clarksville, TN; starts family
1956	Ruth Williams begins her career at Hachland Hill
1969	Husband, Adolf Hach, diagnosed with cancer
1973	First born son, Adolf Hach Jr., passes away; publishes *Love Little Adolf and Yellow Crocus*
1973	Publishes *From Phila with Love, Hachland Hill Recipes: Nashville's Famous Caterer Shares her Secrets*
1974	Publishes *Kountry Kooking*
1975	Publishes *Kitchen Kollege Recipes* (second printing)
1976	Caters UN Luncheon at Centennial Park
1980	Publishes *From Phila with Love* (second printing)
1981	Publishes *Phila Hach's United Nations Cookbook*
1981	Publishes *600 International & Appalachian-Southern Recipes* (*Official Cookbook of 1982 World's Fair*)
1982	World's Fair in Knoxville, TN
1982	Meets Rudy Caduff and establishes connection with Opryland

1983	Publishes *Kountry Kooking For City Folk* (Official Cookbook of Opryland U.S.A.)
1983	Publishes *Plantation Recipes and Kountry Kooking* (Official Cookbook of Opryland U.S.A.)
1983	Publishes *Cracker Barrel Old Country Stores: Old Fashion Intentions*
1983	Publishes *Old Timey Recipes and Proverbs to Live By* (Cracker Barrel Old Country Store Vol I)
1985	Publishes *Tennessee Cooks for Company: Famous Parties, People, Places*
1985	Adolf Hach passes away
1985	Publishes *American Holidays Cookbook* (Cracker Barrel Old Country Store Vol II)
1986	Publishes *Homecoming Cookbook: Famous Parties, People, Places*
1986	Caters the 1986 Tennessee Homecoming (namesake of her book) chaired by Alex Haley and Minnie Pearl
1990	Publishes *Recipes and Health Secrets to Make You Live Longer* (Cracker Barrel Old Country Store Vol III)
1996	Publishes *Global Feasting Tennessee Style*
1999	Publishes *Red Gold Simply Delicious Recipes*
1999	Publishes *Grandmothers Attic Treasures and Scrapbook of Memories*
2005	Leaves Clarksville for Joelton where she grew up and home to Hachland Hill today
2012	Works with Middle Eastern Refugee Women from Nashville's International Center for Employment
2014	Diagnosed with cancer
2015	Recipient of Ruth Fertel Keeper of the Flame Award from Randy Fertel and The Fertel Foundation (SFA Symposium-Phila Ceremony)
2015	Phila passes away

Chapter 1

PARTY-PLEASING
APPETIZERS

Phila's Story

PART 1

PHILA, A THIRD-GENERATION CATERER, was born in 1926 in Joelton, Tennessee, to Arthur and Sophie Rawlings. Her parents, who immigrated from Switzerland, built her childhood home there—it would eventually become a dining venue known as Shadowbrook. The stone building, which is still operated by Phila's sister and her children, was designed to the likeness of a castle in Edinburgh, Scotland. Phila often recounted to me about her time as a child in Joelton, making mud pies decorated with daisies or clover blossoms that she had picked in the field. Her father, the guinea pig for her dirty desserts, pleaded with his wife to supply Phila with some eggs if he was going to have to eat her treats. Phila started using eggs and didn't

Phila's childhood home, Shadowbrook

look back. Her life revolved around the kitchen; she was drawn to the smell and everything else in that space. Her parents and grandparents made their living in the hospitality industry, catering specifically. She was raised to appreciate the hard work and passion that define the service industry. Those same values, which she cultivated from a childhood spent running

This style—no recipes, off-the-cuff—was what she would later dub "country cooking," and it became her calling card.

around a dining-focused inn, were passed on from her to my father and eventually to me, as our family's fifth generation caterer.

At 13 years old, Phila started spending part of her teenage summers in the kitchen of the former Lookout Mountain Hotel, in Chattanooga, Tennessee, where a master chef was in charge. According to Dade County historian, Donna M. Street, Paul Carter and his son, James Inman Carter, began construction of the hotel after purchasing three tracts of land from the Lookout Mountain Land Company in 1927. Directories, on file at the Chattanooga Public Library put President Paul Carter and Vice President/ Treasurer J.l. Carter as the chief operators at the time of its opening in 1928. The 1937 city directory notes S. John Littlegreen as the managing director from then into the middle of the 1950s, the same time interval during which my great grandfather, Arthur Rawlings, was the director of catering.

Phila told me about how, without approval from the hotel's pastry chef (she couldn't recall his name, only that he was French), she was his unwarranted shadow in the kitchen. The pastry chef would throw dough at her in hopes of discouraging her presence, but he eventually gave in and got used to her. Phila watched in awe as the chef baked. He never used any recipes or took any notes, so she decided that she wouldn't do that either. That was how she learned to cook, she explained. This style—no recipes, off-the-cuff—was what she would later dub "country cooking," and it became her calling card. From that point on, her loyalty to the kitchen was steadfast and unmatched. She began baking her beloved sugar biscuits every day, her water rolls twice a day, and for 52 years, she baked four pies a day, coming in at around 76,000 pies over the course of her lifetime.

Phila Hach during her time working at American Airlines

After graduating from Nashville's Harpeth Hall, an all-girls preparatory high school, Phila went on to study at Ward-Belmont College where she earned a degree in music. She had an aptitude for the cello—a detail about her life that not many people know. She then went on to attend Vanderbilt University's Peabody College, while serving as a full-time stewardess for American Airlines. She received her bachelor's degree in foods and nutrition in 1949. Phila attended classes Monday through Thursday and spent Friday, Saturday, and Sunday flying for the airline. She told me that she learned something every day during those years, especially as she broadened her understanding of cultural cuisines during layovers.

On her travels, she would pop into famous kitchens—the Savoy in London, the Georges V in Paris, the Tivoli in Copenhagen, and the Sacher in Vienna—and ask to stage with the chefs. I always tell our guests at Hachland Hill that it must have been a happy-go-lucky time, because those chefs all let her into their kitchens with no reservations. She also sat in on cooking classes at the University of Hawaii on several layovers and learned about the art of cooking Asian and Samoan dishes.

While training flight attendants in Chicago, Phila attended the Antoinette Pope School of Fancy Cooking. During her tenure as a flight attendant, she also stayed at the Prince George Hotel in New York for two years where she wrote the first catering manual for the airline industry before flying to Paris for a weekend at the Georges V hotel. (I wasn't alive to experience it, but when I retell her story, I often joke that airplane food must have been a far more gourmet experience than the one I know today.)

During this particular layover stay at the Georges V, two of her life's greatest journeys took flight. Phila met her future husband, Adolf Hach, a Sorbonne-educated businessman who dealt in the exchange of peat moss and tobacco between Germany and the United States. I never met my grandfather—he was gone too soon for so many—but my siblings and I knew him as "Papa" from stories told to us by my dad and Phila.

(I hadn't dug too far into the Hach family history until a familial name on Instagram piqued my interest in July 2020. I posted a photo on the Hach- land Hill account of a seasonal pastry that received the typical number of likes and comments, but then I saw that a person named Heidi Hach liked the photo. More likes subsequently followed in mere seconds as I imagine she began to scroll through Hachland Hill's gallery. In no time there was a post from her account touting a personal relation to Phila and a deep admiration for her as a fellow pastry chef. I curiously sent a direct message to Heidi wondering if we were distant cousins, joking that we may have both inherited the baking gene in some way or another. She immediately responded that her grandfather, Max Andreas Hach, was the brother of my great grandfather, Julius Adolf Hach. Julius was born in Bremen, Germany, in 1884, and he eventually settled in Clarksville, Tennessee, with his broth- ers; they were there to establish their sides of a family business that was

Phila became the first woman to host a television show in the South, and her assistant, Martha Morman, was one of the first African Americans to appear on television.

rooted in Cuba and Mexico. Heidi Hach Reposteria now lives in Culiacán, Mexico. We exchanged our respective desires to visit each other's businesses in the future, and of course, eat some sweets!)

The other aforementioned fateful occurrence, during that same layover when she met Adolf in Paris, came by way of a telegram from her mother telling her to come back home for something big. Upon the arrival of tele- vision to Nashville in 1950, producers at WSM-TV, per a recommendation from Peabody College, invited her to host a cooking show. Phila became the

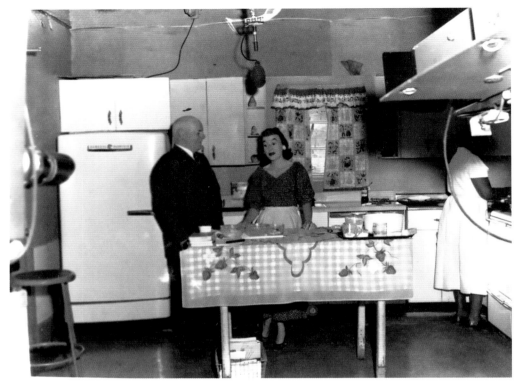

TOP: *Phila on the set of Kitchen Kollege*
BOTTOM LEFT: *On the cover of TV Press*
BOTTOM RIGHT: *Phila with her assistant Martha Morman*

first woman to host a television show in the South, and her assistant, Martha Morman, was one of the first African Americans to appear on television.

On the show, Phila did all of the cooking, but Martha became a second pair of hands to supply whatever was needed during the filming, and to clean up along the way. Martha had been a housekeeper at the news station and Phila remembered the day that she saw her. She insisted on having Martha as an assistant, as a way to give her a better career and to empower another woman like herself. The thirty-minute live show, *Kitchen Kollege,* aired Monday through Friday from 1950 to 1956, with guests including Minnie Pearl, Duncan Hines, and June Carter Cash. (Guests always have a laugh when I give them a Hachland Hill history lesson with breakfast, and joke, "Yes, Duncan Hines was a real person.") Phila published her first cookbook, *Kitchen Kollege Recipes,* in 1954.

Not a storybook "love at first sight" type of romance, Phila and Adolf's initial encounter at the hotel in Paris consisted only of his offer to help with her luggage and her subsequent thank you. Two years later, when he saw her familiar face on WSM-TV's *Kitchen Kollege,* love hit him at second sight. He wrote to her, on more than one occasion, unaware that she would toss his letters into the trashcan without reading them every time. Phila, never knowing whether to call it chance or fate, said that one random day, she rummaged through the garbage pail and salvaged his letter. It was more than a letter she saved that day. She had also salvaged love. Four years of courtship were followed by marriage and a yearlong honeymoon around the world that put both of their careers on hold. Many of the recipes that follow in this chapter honor the love that Phila and Adolf found together.

Phila and Adolf

A TRUE MINT JULEP

MAKES 1 COCKTAIL

TWO THINGS CAN RUIN A JULEP: either too much sugar or too little whiskey. This drink is the "spirit" behind the tale of when Phila smuggled whiskey, with the help of state troopers, into Nashville so that she could serve southern juleps to the United Nations delegation during their 1976 visit. She served the drinks in milk cartons! I worked with a friend of mine, who is the bar manager at Nashville's revered Patterson House, to create this recipe, which pays homage to Phila and her diplomatic julep shenanigans.

1 sprig fresh mint, picked and manicured, plus additional leaves for muddling

2 ounces 100-proof bourbon (use your favorite)

1 ounce demerara syrup

1 dash Woodford Reserve orange bitters

Place a few mint leaves in a silver tumbler and move them around with a bar spoon, rubbing them gently against the bottom and sides of the cup. (Do not over-muddle or crush the mint as it can impart a bitter flavor.) Fill the cup with bourbon, syrup, and bitters. Add crushed ice to fill the cup halfway. With a bar spoon, stir the drink to help dilute it: Place the bar spoon between the palms of your hands and rub hands together using the same motion as if trying to warm them up. Top with more crushed ice. Garnish with fresh mint.

PAPA'S APERTIF

MAKES 16 SERVINGS

APERTIFS, WHICH SEEMINGLY DISAPPEARED IN AMERICA after their initial introduction from European immigrants, are finally finding their prevalence again at craft bars around the country. Phila always touted that my German grandfather, Adolf Hach, who I knew as Papa, was a Sorbonne-educated man with luxurious taste. When they entertained guests at Hachland Hill, devout in his European heritage, Adolf would often complement the meals with apertifs as a starter or palate cleanser. His drink of choice was Dubonnet, and from that, Phila created Adolf's Apertif, which was published in several of her cookbooks. This aperitif is a great start to your dinner party.

1 bottle Dubonnet

1 pint Fords London Dry Gin

1 quart ginger ale

1 dash apricot bitters

Garnish: Twists from 1 Meyer lemon

Place rocks glasses in the freezer for one hour. Mix all ingredients in a large bowl or blender just until foam starts to form, then working in batches, ladle into a stainless-steel cocktail shaker with large ice cubes. Shake vigorously and strain into your frosted rocks glasses. Garnish with lemon twist.

Papa's Apertif pictured on page 30.

A STORIED APERTIF

In a 2011 *New York Times* article, Anistatia Miller, a liquor historian who published *Mixellany Guide to Vermouths and Other Aperitifs*, said, "Americans have been scared of aperitifs, especially vermouths, since Prohibition. When the league of experienced bartenders who were immigrants or first-generation children of immigrants went to war and died or left the U.S. to work in Europe and South America, it left the work pool with people who knew nothing of traditions such as aperitivo." She added that, "Germans, Italians, French, and Spanish émigrés learned to become Americans, rather than embracing their own cultures. They adapted traditions that worked and discarded traditions that made them different." Dubonnet was one of the defining creations from that era. The earliest Dubonnet cocktail recipes were simplistic, equal parts Dubonnet and gin, which made it a standard cocktail during Prohibition.

PLANTER'S PUNCH

SERVES 4

THIS CROWD-PLEASING DRINK PROVIDES WARMTH for chilly bodies while tailgating at a football game in the late fall. I learned this from my time studying at Ole Miss where I admittedly drank my share of punch in the Grove and on the balcony at John Currence's restaurant, Bouré, where he has his own signature Planter's Punch on the menu all year around.

1 cup fresh pineapple juice

½ cup fresh makrut lime juice

½ cup fresh satsuma orange juice

½ cup fresh meyer lemon juice

3 tablespoons grenadine

Dash of Angostura bitters

1 cup Plantation Barbados
    5 Year rum

Garnish: Blood orange slices,
    Luxardo cherries, and
    pineapple sage flower petals

Place several rocks glasses in a freezer to chill. Combine juices with grenadine, bitters, and rum. Pour into chilled glasses over crushed ice. Garnish with orange slices, cherries and flower petals.

Planter's Punch pictured on page 30.

EGGNOG

MAKES 24 SERVINGS

EGGNOG HAS BEEN A GUILTY PLEASURE OF MINE for as long as I can remember. On a visit to Hachland Hill in Clarksville, I once indulged in however-many-is-too-many sips of this custard-like joy, unaware that it was spiked. It was an unpleasant experience to say the least. Nevertheless, my love for eggnog persists to this day. I adapted Phila's recipe with the addition of pineapple sage. The first time I experimented with this herb, which was supplied to me by a local farmer, I fell in love with its unique flavor as an ingredient for sweets and its beautiful flowers as garnishes. I often sell this eggnog by the gallon for delivery around the holidays, and it sells like the custard joy it is!

12 eggs, separated

12 rounded tablespoons sugar

1 teaspoon fresh ground nutmeg, plus more for garnish

1 tablespoon ground pineapple sage leaves and flowers, plus more, whole, to garnish

1 pint Angel's Envy "Port Finish" bourbon

½ pint Old Port rum

2-3 tablespoons Prichard's Sweet Lucy liqueur

1 quart heavy cream, whipped

Beat egg yolks until very light and fluffy. Gradually stir in sugar, followed by the nutmeg and ground pineapple sage. While beating, slowly add bourbon, rum, and liqueur. Fold in whipped cream. Stiffly beat the egg whites and fold into mixture just before serving. Garnish with nutmeg, pineapple sage leaves, and flowers.

Eggnog pictured on page 206.

WASSAIL BOWL

SERVES 8

WASSAILING IS AN ANCIENT CUSTOM derived from England, particularly in cider producing regions. Villagers flocked to their local orchards, reciting songs and incantations out of reverence to the trees with hopes for bountiful harvests in the next year. This practice eventually transformed into people going door to door in song and inviting homeowners to share in a drink from their Wassail Bowl. Today, we know this as caroling. The bowls and particularly their lids, traditionally made from wood, tin, or pottery with multiple handles for shared drinking, were often very ornate and the focal points of festive gatherings. This recipe and its ability to warm the spirits is perfect for winter holidays like Christmas and New Year's Eve.

1 cup water

½ teaspoon fresh nutmeg, ground

½ teaspoon ground ginger

1 stick cinnamon

3 whole cloves

3 allspice berries

2 coriander seeds

2 cardamom seeds

4 lady apples, roasted

1 quart brown ale (I prefer whatever Tailgate Brewery has on its rotating tap)

1 bottle Lustau Deluxe Cream Sherry Capataz Andres

1 cup sugar

6 egg yolks

6 egg whites

Boil the water, then add the spices and roasted apples. Let simmer for exactly 10 minutes. Now add the ale, the bottle of cream sherry, and sugar. (This can vary depending on your taste.) Bring to a boil. Beat egg whites and yolks separately, then fold together. Pour beaten eggs over the hot Wassail and fold over and over to combine. Pass around your loving cup and go and hang your stocking up.

A WASSAILING CAROL

Wassail! wassail! all over the town,
Our toast it is white and our ale it is brown;
Our bowl it is made of the white maple tree;
With the wassailing bowl, we'll drink to thee.

So here is to Broad Mary and to her broad horn
May God send our master a good crop of corn
And a good crop of corn that may we all see
With the wassailing bowl, we'll drink to thee.

COUNTRY QUICHE LORRAINE

SERVES 8

QUICHE IMMEDIATELY MAKES ME THINK OF EASTER WITH PHILA. Whether it was brunch or dinner, she would always serve some sort of quiche as a starting course to round out the already sure-to-be-huge meal. I love her quiche lorraine recipe, which I adapted to reflect some regional influence by way of country ham. My dad usually took care of the hams for our family holidays—from a young age I was eager to learn his process. I eventually inherited the technique to create my own nostalgic dishes at Hachland Hill. Add a little extra hot sauce on top to bring the dish home.

FOR THE BUTTER PASTRY:

1 ½ cups pastry flour

½ teaspoon salt

1 stick unsalted butter

4 tablespoons ice water

FOR THE FILLING:

1 cup grated swiss cheese

4 eggs

2 cups heavy cream

1 tablespoon cornstarch

Pinch of salt

¼ teaspoon garlic powder

Dash of cayenne

1 teaspoon chopped yellow onion

½ cup finely diced cooked
    country ham

Cherry tomatoes, halved

Wild chives

Hot sauce

MAKE THE PASTRY: Combine the flour, salt, and unsalted butter in a food processor until it just starts to resemble a crumb-like texture. Add the iced water through the tube of the processor and pulse until dough comes together. Wrap dough in plastic wrap and chill for one hour. When ready to fill, roll dough out and place in a pie pan. Crimp edges along sides of pan with your fingers to your likeness or use a fork and press down along the edges for an easy fix.

MAKE THE FILLING: Preheat oven to 350 degrees. In a large bowl, combine cheese, eggs, cream, cornstarch, salt, garlic powder, cayenne, onion, and ham, whisking together until incorporated. Pour filling into prepared pie shell. Bake for 25 to 30 minutes. To serve, cut into wedges and garnish with cherry tomatoes and chopped chives. Serve hot sauce on the side.

NASHVILLE HOT CHICKEN CROQUETTES

MAKES 14 TO 20 CROQUETTES (depending on size preference); **SERVES 16**

PHILA'S CHICKEN CROQUETTES WERE A STAPLE OF HER LADIES' LUNCHEONS, which were often hosted on Sundays at Hachland Hill in Clarksville, though the "Nashville Hot" craze hadn't yet taken flight in those years. While I often remark that Nashville Hot renditions, now common of any and every dish imaginable, is hackneyed in our city's restaurants, I do still have a deep, burning love for the taste that Prince's Hot Chicken put on the map for me at a young age. If croquettes aren't your cup of tea, this pulled Nashville Hot Chicken can be thrown on a bun with Sow Good Slaw (page 85) and Garlic-Honey Aïoli (page 232) for a killer sandwich!

FOR THE WET RUB:

4 tablespoons cayenne pepper

⅔ cup olive oil

5 garlic cloves

1 teaspoon salt

1 tablespoon dill weed

1 tablespoon celery seed

FOR THE CHICKEN:

2 whole chickens

Salt and pepper

Wet rub

FOR THE CROQUETTES:

2 cups cream

2 tablespoons butter

4 heaping tablespoons flour

1 teaspoon salt

½ teaspoon celery salt

2 cups pulled chicken

¼ teaspoon cayenne pepper

1 teaspoon parsley

Pinch nutmeg

1 teaspoon lemon juice

1 egg, plus 1 beaten egg

Cracker crumbs for coating

Oil for frying

(continued on next page)

(continued from previous page)

MAKE THE WET RUB: Combine all ingredients in a food processor. Set aside.

PREPARE THE CHICKENS: Preheat oven to 400 degrees. Pat chickens dry and season generously with salt and pepper. Cover completely with wet rub and place in a roasting pan. Roast for about 30 minutes to crisp up the skin. Reduce heat to 350 degrees and continue to cook for an additional 30 minutes, or until the internal temperature of the thigh reads 160 degrees. Remove and set aside until cool enough to handle. Pull meat by hand or fork.

MAKE THE CROQUETTES: Combine cream, butter, and flour in a large saucepan over medium heat. Stir until combined. While still warm, add salt, celery salt, pulled chicken, cayenne, parsley, nutmeg, lemon juice, and egg, stirring well to combine.

Set mixture aside to cool until it becomes very stiff. Shape mixture into croquettes. Dip in beaten egg. Roll in cracker crumbs. In a heavy pan or Dutch oven, heat oil until a pinch of breadcrumbs immediately boils and rises to the top. Fry croquettes in oil until golden brown and very hot.

SALTY DOGS *with* SORGHUM WHIPPED BONE MARROW BUTTER *and* PARSLEY SALAD

SERVES 10

THIS RECIPE IS A FLAVOR BOMB OF A BITE. It starts with the salty dogs, which are crisp, cigar-shaped crackers, that get topped with whipped bone marrow and a bite of parsley salad. Go to your local butcher and ask for the bones to be cut into canoes if you do not have ability to do so yourself. My first house was right around the corner from my favorite butcher shop, Bare Bones Butcher in the Nations, which was maybe a blessing or a curse depending on whether you asked my taste buds or my waistline.

FOR THE SALTY DOGS:

2 cups all-purpose flour

1 teaspoon baking soda

½ teaspoon salt

1 package dry onion soup (I use Knorr)

½ cup Crisco

¼ cup apple cider vinegar

½ cup whole milk

Caraway seeds

Coarse salt

FOR THE BONE MARROW BUTTER:

8 marrowbones, cut in half lengthwise

Salt and pepper to taste

½ cup softened unsalted butter

2 tablespoons sorghum

1 tablespoon garlic powder

FOR THE PARSLEY SALAD:

1 bunch flat-leaf parsley, picked and chopped

¼ cup capers

2 tablespoons extra-virgin olive oil

¼ teaspoon lemon zest

Juice of 1 lemon

½ red onion, diced

1 teaspoon minced garlic

Chili oil to garnish

Micro greens to garnish

(continued on next page)

(continued from previous page)

MAKE THE SALTY DOGS: Preheat oven to 275 degrees. Combine flour, baking soda, salt, and dry onion soup mix. Work in Crisco with fingers. Add vinegar to whole milk and combine all at once with dry ingredients. Shape dough into small finger shapes and roll lightly in salt and caraway seeds. Bake until brown and crisp.

MAKE THE BONE MARROW BUTTER: Raise oven temperature to 420 degrees. On a parchment-lined baking sheet, spread bones marrow-side up. Sprinkle with kosher salt and pepper. Bake for 15 to 20 minutes until marrow is bubbly and gelatinous. Set bones aside until cool enough to handle. Reserve rendered beef fat from baking sheet. Scrape the bone marrow into a food processor. Add the remaining ingredients. While pulsing everything together, slowly pour the rendered beef fat through the tube until the mixture is smooth and spreadable. Refrigerate until ready to use.

MAKE THE PARSLEY SALAD: In a large bowl, toss together the parsley, capers, olive oil, lemon zest and juice, onion, and garlic. To serve, dab a pat of marrow butter onto a salty dog and sprinkle with a pinch of the salad, a bit of chili oil, and the micro greens. Serve at once.

PHILA'S (HIGHFALUTIN) HOBO SANDWICHES

SERVES 8

PHILA'S HOBO SANDWICHES, A RECIPE NEAR AND DEAR TO HER HEART on account of Mr. Jemerson (see story on page 49), was printed in several of her cookbooks. Her pastry ingredients consisted of three cups of flour, one and one-quarter cups mayonnaise, and the juice of half an orange. Her filling included potato, turnip, onion, one pound of ground beef, and half a pound of ground pork. In keeping with the elevated southern cuisine that I serve at Hachland Hill today, I gave a facelift to her frugal delights with the substitution of croissant dough, smoked bologna, and smoked cheddar cheese. We'll call these Phila's High-falutin Hobo Sandwiches. They go great with Sorghum BBQ Sauce (page 233) or Heirloom Tomato Jam (page 61).

570 grams Croissant dough (page 179)

2 small raw potatoes, sliced thin

2 small raw turnips, sliced thin

1 medium onion, sliced thin and halved

1 ½ pounds ground smoked bologna (I use Gifford's, which is local to Nashville)

1 cup smoked cheddar cheese, shredded

1 whole egg

1 egg yolk

Pinch of salt

Roll the dough into a rectangle measuring 8-by-16 inches. Refrigerate and let dough rest for 15 minutes. Using a paring knife, mark the dough halfway along the 8-inch side of the rectangle. Cut small marks every 2 inches along the longer side of the dough. Cut triangles starting from the side with the 4-inch markings. Alternatively use a croissant cutter and roll it on the dough to create your triangles. Make a ½-inch cut at the base of each triangle.

(continued on next page)

PHILA'S (HIGHFALUTIN) HOBO SANDWICHES

(continued from previous page)

Set a proofing cabinet to 72 to 78 degrees. Preheat oven to 350 degrees. Place 2 potato slices, 2 turnip slices, 1 onion slice at the base of each pastry triangle right in front of the slits. Place a small scoop of the ground bologna over the vegetable slices and top with 2 tablespoons cheese.

Whisk together egg, yolk, and salt in a small bowl. Brush the tip of each dough triangle with egg wash. Fold the inside corners into the center of the triangle and roll the dough toward the tip of the triangle, so that the filling is completely wrapped in dough. Make sure that the tip is on the underside of the shaped croissant. Place the croissants on a parchment-lined baking sheet, about 2 inches apart. Curl the sides of the croissant together so that they form a crescent. Place the croissants in the proofing cabinet for 45 to 60 minutes, or until doubled in size.

Brush the croissants with the remaining egg wash, completely covering the exposed surfaces but not allowing the egg wash to drip or pool. Be careful and brush lightly as to not puncture the dough and deflate the croissants. Bake for 15 to 20 minutes, or until medium golden brown. Remove the croissants from the oven and let cool on the baking sheet. Serve immediately or within one day.

PHILA'S (HIGHFALUTIN) HOBO SANDWICHES

THE STORY OF MR. JEMERSON

Phila's "open door" philosophy spanned beyond her Sunday Night Suppers. The story's point of origin is a heartwarming tale that began with the construction of Hachland Hill.

Phila once told me how she used to see a man walk by her home with his feet half out of his shoes. She would wave to him every time. One day, after two or three years, he walked up the hill to the house. She told me that he had the jitters because he was always drunk. He wanted to know what Hachland Hill was, so she invited him in for coffee.

Adolf, recognizing this man as someone who lived under a nearby bridge with seven other men, berated Phila for inviting him into their home and demanded to know what she was thinking. She told him that she was feeding a man, drinking coffee, and having a wonderful conversation.

"Adolf said 'That's a derelict. He's an alcoholic that lives under the bridge,'" Phila told me. "I said, 'Oh, how wonderful.'"

Later that morning, she looked out and saw the man raking all of their leaves. "He stayed with me until he died, and I was the one that went down to put him in the basement at Tarper's Funeral Home. Me and all of his little derelict friends," she told me.

Phila described Mr. Jemerson as a real part of her life, a family member in the same right as Ruth Williams.

Life is about give and take, according to her, and not being judgmental in its dealings. "Give from other people and take from other people, attitudes and ideas. You receive in the same debt as you can give," she said.

WELSH RAREBIT

SERVES 8

ONE OF MY FAVORITE HELP-YOURSELF DISHES IS WELSH RAREBIT, or Welsh rabbit as it once sounded to my young mind. (Rabbit may have been part of its earliest form but there is not much certainty in this. It has been proposed that the word, rarebit, is a corruption of the dish "welsh rabbit" having been recorded in 1725 and a mutated name from 1785 by Francis Grose.) My mom made this humble childhood favorite, often on the night next to a big holiday—it was a nice alternative to the hell storm of cooking and dishes that came in the day before or after. We would have it with crackers, pickles, and leftover Christmas ham. Her grandmother used to tell her that the trick is to put the thickening in at the very beginning.

2 eggs

1 ½ cups whole milk

½ teaspoon red pepper

1 teaspoon salt

1 tablespoon Worcestershire sauce

3 tablespoons ketchup

1 pound sharp cheese, diced

1 heaping tablespoon cornstarch dissolved in ¼ cup water

Crackers for serving (page 249)

Dill pickles

Raw onion rings

Pickle relish

In a heat-proof bowl, beat eggs. Add milk, seasonings, and diced cheese and place bowl on top of a double boiler over medium-low heat. Add dissolved cornstarch. Stir often. It should be similar in consistency to yogurt. If too thin, add additional cornstarch; if too thick, cut with a little milk. Once melted and combined, serve accompanied by crackers, dill pickles, raw onion rings, and pickle relish.

COUNTRY HAM PÂTÉ
on BEATEN BISCUITS

SERVES 10

PHILA, WHO HAD MORE VARIATIONS OF BISCUIT RECIPES in her combined cookbooks than I can count on two hands, taught me the basics of scratch biscuits when I was a young boy sitting on the counter beside her at Hachland Hill in Clarksville. Ruth Williams, prior to her retirement, supplied my refresher courses. She tried to teach a chef, who had been hired to run the kitchen before I found my place at the helm of the rolling pin—but he wasn't the right fit. "I showed him how to do it, and I watched him," Ruth told me. "But somehow this boy keeps making hockey pucks. Carter, you're going to have to make the biscuits," she told me. I eventually fine-tuned my biscuit abilities when I studied pastry and bread at the International Culinary Center in New York City, learning French technique from Chris Ciresi who was the former executive pastry chef at Manhattan's legendary Plaza Hotel before becoming an instructor. The key to these biscuits is how you beat them. I include instructions for using a bread break—which is a hand operated device used for kneading bread or biscuit dough—but you can also do it by hand. As Phila once said, you have to do it "over and over until the dough starts talking back to you."

BEATEN BISCUITS

7 cups all-purpose flour, sifted

1 teaspoon baking powder

1 teaspoon salt

4 tablespoons sugar

1 cup hog lard or 2 ½ sticks unsalted butter

1 ⅓ cups whole milk, cold

Preheat oven to 350 degrees.

Sift together flour, baking powder, salt, and sugar. Repeat two more times. Using your fingers, cut the lard into the dry ingredients until the mixture is very fine. Stir in the cold milk to make a stiff dough.

(continued on next page)

COUNTRY HAM PÂTÉ ON BEATEN BISCUITS

(continued from previous page)

If using a bread break, roll the dough into a ball, flatten it out, and start running it through the machine. Fold dough in half and run it back through the machine. Continue until the dough is flat, about 15 to 20 minutes by machine. If doing this by hand, roll the dough out, flatten it, and fold and re-roll the dough over and over again until it's beat out flat. It will take about 30 minutes by hand.

Finally, roll out the dough to ½-inch thickness. Cut biscuits with a circular cutter and prick each with a fork in several spots. Be sure to prick all the way through as this holds the flaky layers together.

Bake for 25 minutes. Serve with Country Ham Pâté.

COUNTRY HAM PÂTÉ

1 pound country ham

1 pot strong coffee

2 small garlic cloves

1 tablespoon prepared horseradish

1 cup mayonnaise

2 tablespoons Dijon mustard

1 teaspoon white pepper

2 tablespoons dry sherry

2 tablespoons fresh dill, finely chopped

Pickled jalapeños

Cornichons

Dice the country ham. Place in a sauté pan and pour in just enough strong coffee to cover the ham. Cook over medium heat until the meat is warmed through. Drain the ham, discard the coffee, and pat ham dry. In a food processor, combine ham, garlic, and horseradish and pulse until a paste forms. Add the mayonnaise, mustard, white pepper, and sherry. Pulse to combine. Transfer mixture to a bowl, fold in fresh dill, and refrigerate until ready to serve. To serve, place pâté in a jar and serve accompanied by the beaten biscuits, pickled jalapeños, and cornichons.

BEEF TENDERLOIN ROLLS *with* GARLIC CHIVE HORSERADISH CREAM

SERVES 8 TO 12

I KNOW EXACTLY WHICH TWO RECIPES I FIRST MADE WITH PHILA. Chocolate nut drop cookies and apple crepes with vanilla-bourbon sauce. Something about cracking eggs and dough-covered fingers were great fun for me as a child. Savory applications with her came a little later in life; maybe because with meats comes knives and butchery, which both require a little more maturity and steadier hands. Beef tenderloin and leg of lamb were the first two cuts of meats that we tackled together. Her tenderloin was a family favorite and a staple at Hachland Hill. It still is today. She would make it for every family holiday, along with her rolls and twice-baked potatoes. Those three things are a match made in heaven. She would only use salt and pepper on her tenderloin, that was it, and it was simplicity at its finest. I now use locally sourced beef for the iconic dish at Hachland Hill, and I prepare it with just a slight variation of her recipe. My brother, who always regarded her tenderloin and potatoes as his favorite meal, admitted to favoring my tenderloin at the holidays since her passing. I had a good teacher.

A NOTE ON PROOFING: A lot of newer ovens have a proofing preset, but proofing until dough is doubled in size can also be achieved by letting the rolls sit at room temperature covered in plastic wrap. If you want to give them some color and crust, make an egg wash by whisking together one egg, one egg yolk, and a pinch of salt; brush the rolls right before baking.

FOR THE BEEF TENDERLOIN:

1 (4-5 pound) whole beef
    tenderloin

Salt

Pepper

Garlic powder

1 tablespoon Maggi seasoning

FOR THE BRIOCHE ROLLS:

Brioche dough (page 174)

¼ cup melted unsalted butter

FOR THE GARLIC CHIVE HORSERADISH CREAM:

2 cups mayonnaise

¼ cup sour cream

½ cup garlic chives

2 small garlic cloves

Prepared horseradish to taste

1 teaspoon salt

1 teaspoon smoked paprika

Pea shoot tendrils to garnish

(continued on next page)

BEEF TENDERLOIN ROLLS WITH
GARLIC CHIVE HORSERADISH CREAM

(continued from previous page)

MAKE THE BEEF TENDERLOIN: Remove the chain and the silver skin from the tenderloin. (This can be done for you by a local butcher.) Tie tenderloin with butcher's twine. Rub generously with salt and pepper, then sprinkle with garlic powder and rub that in as well. Let rest in the refrigerator overnight.

The next day, preheat the oven to 350 degrees. Place tenderloin on a roasting rack on a baking sheet. Sprinkle Maggi evenly over top of tenderloin. Roast in oven for about 45 minutes for medium rare. Remove from oven and let rest. Cut off the twine. Slice tenderloin to desired thickness. If there is any excess blood, let it run off and pat dry. Wrap meat and refrigerate until ready to assemble rolls.

MAKE THE BRIOCHE ROLLS: Preheat oven to 350 degrees. Shape brioche dough into 20- to 30-gram rounds or squares. Set on a baking tray and proof at 75 to 80 degrees for 45 minutes to 1 hour, or until doubled in size. Place rolls in a preheated oven for 15 minutes. Remove from oven and immediately brush with melted butter.

MAKE THE GARLIC CHIVE HORSERADISH CREAM: Combine mayonnaise, sour cream, garlic chives, garlic, and prepared horseradish in a food processor. Pulse until smooth. Season with salt and smoked paprika.

TO ASSEMBLE: Cut rolls in half and spread garlic chive horseradish cream on the bottoms. Place one slice of tenderloin on top of the cream and garnish with a pinch of pea shoot tendrils. Close the rolls and you have a party pleaser!

HOECAKE TRIO

SERVES 12 TO 16

I FIRST LEARNED HOW TO MAKE HOECAKES under the tutelage of Ruth Williams. She learned them from Phila and taught them to me with the same simple, yet vague, directions that were passed on to her: "Yellow meal with just enough sugar, but don't make it too sweet. Mix that with just enough eggs to make it grits consistency, but don't make it too soupy. Fry them up with this skillet and that spatula, never use another. Flip them once, and they're done when they're done." I adapted the recipe to include some buttermilk, flour, corn, and garlic. At Hachland Hill, we serve my corn hoecakes as hors d'oeuvres for wedding cocktail hours and during dinner with our appointment guests. I like to line up two hoecakes next to each other, piping pimento cheese onto one garnished with house pickle relish, and spreading the other with half tomato jam and half country pesto topped off with seasonal microgreens. It's also fun to serve the three spreads separately beside the hoecakes—what I call southern tapas style at Hachland Hill—so guests can create their own flavorful bite.

NOTE: If you want an extra element of freshness, you can make your own pimentos by rubbing two whole red bell peppers with olive oil and roasting them for about 15 minutes in a 350-degree oven, or until they just start to relax and blister. Remove from oven and let cool. Pull the tops off gently with your finger or a fork, then removed the seed pod. Dice the peppers and you have your fresh pimentos.

(continued on next page)

(continued from previous page)

CORN KERNEL HOECAKES

MAKES 20 HOECAKES

5 eggs

2 cups yellow cornmeal

1 cup all-purpose flour

¼ cup sugar

¼ teaspoon garlic powder

1 cup corn kernels, whole

½ cup buttermilk

Vegetable oil

In a large bowl, whisk eggs, then add the cornmeal, flour, sugar, garlic powder, corn, and buttermilk. Continue to whisk until smooth (the consistency of grits). In a skillet over medium heat, add oil. Ladle rounds of batter into the skillet allowing space between each round. After about 3 minutes, or until they are crisp enough to handle from the bottom, flip the cakes and let fry for a few more minutes until done. Remove and place on a wire rack or paper towels, which will absorb the excess grease.

PIMENTO CHEESE

MAKES ABOUT 4 CUPS

1 cup cream cheese

2 cups extra sharp cheddar

2 cups sharp cheddar

1 ½ cups mayonnaise

¼ teaspoon garlic powder

¼ teaspoon cayenne

1 teaspoon salt

1 teaspoon white pepper

1 tablespoon mustard powder

½ cup diced pimentos

1 jalapeño, seeded and finely diced

2 tablespoons chopped fresh dill

In a stand mixer fit with a paddle attachment, cream the three cheeses together. Add the mayonnaise and dry ingredients and mix until evenly incorporated. Using a rubber spatula, fold in the pimentos, jalapeño, and dill. Let chill in the refrigerator for 2 hours before serving.

(continued on next page)

(continued from previous page)

COUNTRY PESTO

MAKES ABOUT 1 QUART

1 bunch turnip greens, center ribs and stems removed

1 bunch of collard greens, center ribs and stems removed

1 bunch mustard greens, center ribs and stems removed

Kosher salt

1 country ham hock

½ cup picked fresh lovage leaves

2 cups extra-virgin olive oil

1 cup toasted pecans

8 tablespoons apple cider vinegar

2 teaspoons honey

1 teaspoon crushed red pepper flakes

Cracked peppercorn

Rinse the greens. Place in a strainer and shower with kosher salt, moving leaves around to distribute the salt evenly. Strain. Rinse, salt, and strain again; repeating this process a total of 4 times. Cook the greens in a large pot of salted, boiling water. Add the country ham hock and simmer until tender and you are able to scrape its meat away from the bone with ease. Drain greens and transfer to bowl of ice water. (You can reserve the hock to shred and mix in with greens as a side dish.) Once chilled, drain greens again and pat dry with paper towels. In a food processor, blend together the greens, lovage, oil, pecans, vinegar, honey, and crushed red pepper until a coarse puree forms. If it is too stiff, slowly pour more oil through the top while pulsing to achieve desired consistency. Season with salt and cracked peppercorn to taste, then let sit in the refrigerator to settle before serving.

HEIRLOOM TOMATO JAM

MAKES ABOUT 1 QUART

5 pounds purple cherokee tomatoes (or you can substitute any red tomato)

2 pounds sugar

½ teaspoon salt

1 orange, thinly sliced

1 lemon, thinly sliced

1 (3-inch) stick cinnamon

1 (4-inch) piece ginger, peeled

2 cups seedless raisins

½ cup lemon juice

1 tablespoon balsamic vinegar

¼ teaspoon Tabasco sauce

Peel tomatoes and chop. In a saucepan, combine tomatoes with sugar, salt, orange, and lemon. Stir over medium heat until sugar dissolves. Add cinnamon and ginger and bring to a boil; reduce heat and cook over low until thick, about 1 hour, stirring occasionally.

Remove cinnamon and ginger. Add raisins and lemon juice and bring back to a boil. Stir in vinegar and Tabasco, pour into half-pint jars, and seal at once.

END OF THE RAINBOW BITES

SERVES 12

MY DAD AND A GANG OF HIS CLOSEST FRIENDS have taken an annual trout fishing trip to the White River in Arkansas—dubbed "The Freeze Out"—every February for more than four decades. I felt so abandoned whenever he left for a fishing or hunting trip with the guys when I was younger, but was always happy to see him come home as I could count on having a few birds or fish to clean and cook up with him upon his return. This recipe is inspired by that bond and all of the trips that he took my brother Joseph and me on once we were of age. I call for a lemon pepper and black sesame seed blend as the perfect complement to season these bagels but feel free to use any seasoning you'd like. Today, I source our rainbow trout from the Bucksnort Trout Ranch about an hour down the interstate from Hachland Hill.

LEMON PEPPER AND BLACK SESAME SEED BAGEL BITES

MAKES 1 DOZEN BAGELS

7 ¼ cups bread flour

2 cups water

¼ cup sugar

2 tablespoons malt

1 ¾ tablespoons fresh yeast

3 ½ teaspoons salt

Lemon pepper and black sesame seed blend

Combine the bread flour, water, sugar, malt, and yeast in the bowl of a stand mixer fitted with a hook attachment. Mix on medium speed for about 5 minutes. Add the salt and continue mixing for 7 minutes more, or until dough comes together. Portion the dough into 50-gram pieces and shape into batards. Cover the batards and let rest for 15 minutes. Shape each batard into a ring and place on a sheet pan. Cover loosely with plastic wrap to allow room for rising. Refrigerate overnight.

(continued on next page)

(continued from previous page)

The next day, preheat the oven to 425 degrees. Bring a skillet of water to a boil on the stove. In groups of four or five depending on the size of your skillet, place each bagel into the boiling water for 5 to 10 seconds, flipping them once during that time. Quickly fish out the bagels with tongs or a fork and immediately place them onto a parchment-lined baking sheet. Dust with the lemon pepper and black sesame blend. Place the bagels in the oven for 12 minutes to finish cooking. Remove and let cool.

FOR THE TARE SAUCE:

1 cup soy sauce

¼ cup sake

1 cup mirin

½ cup dark brown sugar

2 tablespoons rice wine vinegar

1 (2-inch) piece of ginger, peeled and smashed

2 garlic cloves, peeled and smashed

1 tablespoon whole black peppercorns

3 scallions, chopped

FOR THE FILLING:

3 whole smoked rainbow trout

½ cup plain yogurt

½ cup cream cheese

½ cup unsalted butter

2 tablespoons extra-virgin olive oil

1 egg yolk

Juice of 1 lemon

¼ teaspoon lime zest

1 teaspoon fresh dill

1 teaspoon white pepper

1 tablespoon chopped garlic chives

1 tablespoon real wasabi powder

Lemon Pepper and Black Sesame Seed Bagel Bites

1 bunch watercress

1 watermelon radish, thinly shaved

½ cucumber, thinly shaved

MAKE THE TARE SAUCE: In a saucepan, whisk together all ingredients over a medium-low heat until smooth. Bring to a boil, then back down to a simmer until it reduces by half and is thick enough to coat the back of a spoon, about 20 minutes. Strain the solids and let the tare cool. Chill in an airtight container in the refrigerator until you're ready to unleash the umami.

MAKE THE FILLING: Remove the trout meat from the carcass, making sure there are no hidden bones in the bowl. In a stand mixer fitted with a paddle attachment, mix together the yogurt, cream cheese, unsalted butter, and trout meat. Replace the paddle with the whisk attachment. Gradually drizzle in the olive oil followed by the egg yolk, lemon juice, lime zest, dill, pepper, chives, and wasabi powder. Whisk until evenly incorporated.

TO ASSEMBLE: Spread filling onto bagel bites and garnish with watercress, radish, and cucumber. Drizzle the tare sauce over top.

Chapter 2

SOUPS & SALADS

Phila's Story
PART 2

PHILA AND ADOLF MOVED TO CLARKSVILLE, TENNESSEE, in 1956, where they opened a catering business and their first hospitality venture, Hachland Hill Inn. They welcomed their first son, Adolf Jr. Hach, who was born severely mentally and physically handicapped in that same year. Their second son, my father Joe Hach, followed shortly after in 1959. Phila, worn out after so much travel and television, said that she was ready to come home. She told me years later that regardless of where you roam in this world, "home is where your heart is." Adolf, meanwhile, was occupied with his import/export business, which Phila said was a poison that she knew she picked when she married him. He was usually away, and busy with his work for the Rudolph-Hach Tobacco Company, but she needed help at Hachland Hill. Later, Phila told me with affection, "that was when Adolf sent me 'my Ruthie.'"

Ruth Williams was the backbone of Hachland Hill. She was the lead cook, the housekeeper, and the dishwasher. If she wasn't shaping rolls, she was mopping the ballroom, flipping bedrooms, or wearing one of her other many hats. While Phila did all of the intricate tasks, like decorating cakes, Ruth fried chicken, prepped the greens, and made the hoecakes. Ruth taught me later that the small tedious tasks in the kitchen are performed

Phila with her sons Adolf Jr. and Joe

Carter Hach and Ruth Williams

by its most valuable and dedicated member. It's the reason why, today, I never ask anything of anyone that I wouldn't do myself. I love hopping in to help with dishes or blowing leaves off the grounds if it makes someone else's load just a bit lighter. It's an aptitude that many service industry workers can appreciate. Phila would do all of those things too, of course, but everyone needs a Ruth to keep the show running when work gets busy.

Ruth was the one who schooled me in a lot of Hachland Hill's Southern staples, such as fried chicken, hoecakes, and greens, before handing over the torch upon her retirement. Ruth told me, during her first year, she often cried behind closed doors when Phila fussed at her, thinking it wasn't going to work, but she reminded herself that she needed the work and joked about not being one for factories. Phila, who was very outspoken, said Ruth told it like it was no matter the circumstances. "Ruth was here today and told me that I made her cry many times. I didn't mean to and never saw it," Phila told me. "She's my confidant. She knows more about me than I know about myself. She's never been a day late in her life, which is a great attribute, and she would do anything for my sons. She's a wonderful friend." Ruth worked for two more years after Phila's passing before she retired on her eightieth birthday in 2017. Remarkably, she still stops by from time to time to help with slow-paced catering prep, like wrapping rolls for boxed meals.

LEFT: *Phila and Adolf hosting Sunday Night Supper*
RIGHT: *Phila with Julia Child*

During its renowned "Sunday Night Suppers," Hachland Hill was visited by an extensive list of personalities from all different walks of life, including Julia Child, General William Westmoreland, Roy Acuff, and Oprah Winfrey. Phila allowed my dad to invite his peers, and she and Adolf asked whoever they wanted to attend, and then they had what she called an open-door policy. She told me that anybody, even if she hadn't met them, could call and say they were coming. Drunk or sober, it didn't matter, because she saw everyone as her friend.

Otherwise, dining at Hachland Hill was by appointment only and guests chose their dinner when the reservation was made. Aside from the family living quarters and the formal dining room, the Spanish Colonial home included a garden room for brunch, a ball room, terrace room, and four 1790 log houses scattered about the grounds for those guests seeking solitude from the hectic main inn, which was almost literally a zoo. Aside from guests, Phila and Adolf had ten peacocks, an emu, two rheas, an alligator, two spider monkeys, a woolly monkey, an Afghan hound, two white German shepherds, two great danes, and a handful of ducks. On one occasion, Phila remembers Adolf receiving a phone call informing him that the peacocks had fled Hachland Hill and had made their way onto the roof of a nearby hospital, where they were accused of disturbing patients.

"Don't take any wooden nickels," was a frequent advisory phrase from Phila, and one that she abided by in her own life. This colloquialism, a staple of household Southern slang, surfaced into general use long before the circulation of wooden coins that were typical counterfeit ruses on innocent small-town tourists visiting big cities. The adage, simply put, is a suggestion to be cautious in one's dealings. I think someone who embraces life with no reservations and lives it for the moment, always exercising prudence before naivety, is extraordinary. There is no denying that was how Phila lived.

In 1969, Adolf was diagnosed with throat cancer and received a laryngectomy and survived. In 1973, five days before his birthday, Adolf Jr. passed away. He was 16 years old. In the months following his departure, Phila authored a book titled *Love Little Adolf and Yellow Crocus* to commemorate her first-born son. This loss hit her as hard as any would for a mother of a child taken so young in life. She buried that feeling in her brain with sweet thoughts saved for later mourning on account of an event that was happening at Hachland Hill in the midst of it all.

Ruth, who said she never saw Phila cry in their 60 years together, reflected on that day to me. "Mr. Hach was at the hospital, and I was working a wedding with Miss Phila when she got the news of Little Adolf's passing," Ruth said. "She didn't want any sympathy and made sure the bride didn't find out. That's her strength in character: not wanting to ruin someone else's special day on account of her own misfortune."

I think someone who embraces life with no reservations and lives it for the moment, always exercising prudence before naivety, is extraordinary. There is no denying that was how Phila lived.

Thinking back to the wooden nickel adage and the phrase's broader concept of keeping oneself composed in life's unfortunate dealings, rather than its literal warning to elude scams, Phila hurdled many pains among her prosperities, always marching forward. She always had an "open door," and she was always ready to embrace the next step in her journey, whatever came her way. Twelve years later, after another diagnosis, Phila lost her husband Adolf to lung cancer in 1985.

JOSEPH'S VEGETABLE STEW

SERVES 8

WHILE OUR CULTURE HAS BECOME OBSESSED with the allure of supplements—pre-workout, during a workout, post-workout, pill throughout the day—Phila used to say, about Joseph's Vegetable Soup, that a person could feel the vitamins sliding down their throat.

"Look at then, and look at now. Things are best simple," she said. "How can you improve on a can of Prego and vegetables, and adding whatever you want to the mix?"

The signature soup was named for my big brother, Joseph Hach Jr., who sat on the counter beside her stove in 1996 and came up with this recipe, making his own contribution to her cookbook of that year. On cold winter days, I often make this hearty soup with the addition of venison to surprise our retreat guests at noon with something full of warmth.

1 jar Prego chunky spaghetti sauce

1 (14 ½ ounce) can whole kernel corn

1 (14 ½ ounce) can green beans

1 (14 ½ ounce) can lima beans

1 (14 ½ ounce) can cut sweet potatoes

1 (14 ½ ounce) can sliced beets

1 (14 ½ ounce) can mixed vegetables

1 (14 ½ ounce) can sliced okra

1 tablespoon olive oil (optional)

1 pound ground venison (optional)

Put all ingredients in a large pot and simmer together for 30 minutes.

If adding the venison: In a large cast-iron skillet, heat olive oil over medium heat for about 2 minutes until hot. Add ground venison and use a spatula to press it into an even, flat layer in the pan. Let cook untouched for 5 minutes. Remove venison from skillet, straining off any excess oil. Add it along with the other ingredients to the pot before simmering.

CRACKER BALL SOUP

SERVES 5

I DON'T KNOW THE EXACT HISTORY OF THIS RECIPE, which Phila printed in several of her cookbooks, but I do know it is easy and a crowd pleaser. My best iteration would be to call this a country spin on Jewish soup dumplings, better known as matzoh ball soup. I feel sure that Phila was working the classic recipe, which calls for matzoh meal, and thought to herself, "I'm going to make it with crackers and lots of salt, then it will be my own original invention. Cracker ball soup, yes. This is what I'll call it!"

4 eggs

3 tablespoons chicken fat

4 half eggshells of water

Salt and pepper, to taste (Phila preferred a heavy helping of salt)

1 dash nutmeg

2 cups cracker crumbs

2 quarts chicken broth

½ cup fresh parsley, chopped

Beat eggs, then add chicken fat and water, salt and pepper to taste, and nutmeg. Stir in enough cracker crumbs to make a stiff dough. Shape into small balls. Bring chicken broth to a boil and season generously with parsley. Drop cracker balls into boiling broth and let simmer for 30 minutes.

WILD DUCK *and* WHITE BEAN SOUP

SERVES 10

BACON-WRAPPED CHUNKS OF DUCK BREAST with jalapeño and cream cheese were a normal snack in my youth. I learned that this was the case for many young duck hunters when I got to Ole Miss and found that this was the one thing my comrades seemed to know how to make with their spoils during duck season. Later, I wondered why this was the only dish being made from such a beautiful bird and began experimenting with other recipes from my grandmother and favorite wild game cookbooks. I remember digging a three-foot-deep pit behind my house during my junior year to smoke ducks for a flatbread. After a lot of R&D, I created a simple dish that is perfect after a cold day duck hunting. Serve these with Corn Kernel Hoecakes (page 59) .

2 cups dried white beans

2 wild ducks

Salt

Pepper

1 cup rendered pork fat

½ pound lean ham, diced

1 bay leaf

3 sprigs parsley, chopped

1 large yellow onion

½ pod cayenne pepper

½ quart ham stock*

1 gallon boiling water

2 tablespoons bacon, chopped

*NOTE: This can be made by simmering ham bones in water for six hours.

Rinse the dried beans and add to a bowl, along with 8 cups water, and soak overnight. The next day, drain and rinse the beans. Clean the ducks and cut into 8 bone-in pieces. Generously season the pieces with salt and pepper. In a pot, heat the pork fat over medium heat and brown the duck pieces on every side. Add the remaining ingredients, except the beans, and simmer for 2 hours. Add beans, folding them into the soup, and continue to simmer for 1 more hour until duck falls from the bone. Remove bones before serving.

CHICKEN & DUMPLINS

MAKES 5 SERVINGS

THIS WAS ONE OF MY BROTHER'S FAVORITE THINGS TO SCARF DOWN after a long day of arrowhead hunting, flipping up stones for crawdads, and catching minnows in our makeshift nets. Phila would whip it up in no time as soon as she'd see us walking up to the door in our soaked clothes and sandals full of grit from the creek bed. Simplicity at its finest!

FOR THE CHICKEN:

1 fat hen

1 handful of parsley, chopped

1 large carrot, peeled and cut into medium-sized pieces

1 dash poultry seasoning

Salt and pepper to taste

FOR THE DUMPLINGS:

2 cups flour

4 teaspoons baking powder

½ teaspoon salt

2 teaspoons butter

⅔ cup whole milk, plus a little extra

MAKE THE CHICKEN AND BROTH: Place hen in a large saucepot. Add parsley, carrot, and poultry seasoning. Add a sprinkling of salt and pepper, then cover with water. Simmer slowly until tender, about 4 hours. Pull chicken away from bones and discard them, reserving the chicken meat in a shallow bowl with enough broth to cover it. Strain and reserve remaining broth for dumplings.

MAKE THE DUMPLINGS: Sift together the dry ingredients. Work in the butter with the tips of your fingers. Add milk gradually. Roll the dough out to ¼-inch thickness. Cut into 1- by 2-inch strips. In a stockpot, bring broth to a simmer. Drop dumplings into hot broth and cook for 8 to 10 minutes. Add reserved chicken and broth to the dumplings and stir together.

TURKS TURBAN SOUP

SERVES 8

TURBAN SQUASH ONCE CAUGHT MY EYE during peak pumpkin season. Why, you ask? It looks like an enchanted pumpkin! I played around with a few recipes, eventually running an impromptu soup for an October rehearsal dinner. It received several "oohs" and "ahhs" as a first course and it's become a staple for rehearsal dinner offerings ever since.

2 turban squash, seeded and peeled

4 tablespoons melted butter

3 garlic cloves, minced

4 medium carrots, peeled and diced, plus 1 peeled and saved, for garnish

2 sweet potatoes, peeled and diced

7 cups chicken stock

1 cup cream

1 tablespoon fresh dill, finely chopped

1 tablespoon fresh sage, finely chopped

Salt and pepper to taste

¼ cup balsamic reduction for garnish

Baby red vein sorrel for garnish

Scoop out the meat from the squash. In a large saucepan, heat the butter over medium heat. Add the squash meat, garlic, carrots, and sweet potato, and cook for 5 minutes. Add the stock, cover, and simmer for 30 minutes or until vegetables are tender. Once tender, transfer vegetables and broth to a food processor and puree. While blending, pour cream through the top of the processor. Return mixture to saucepan and stir in the dill and sage. Season to taste with salt and pepper. Simmer on low heat for 10 minutes, stirring constantly until ready to serve. Drizzle with balsamic reduction and garnish with baby red vein sorrel and shaved carrot.

BRUNSWICK STEW

SERVES 8

HUMORIST, ROY BLOUNT JR., WROTE "Brunswick Stew is what happens when small mammals carrying ears of corn fall into barbeque pits." Phila often used chicken in place of small game when she made this stew, which can be traced back to 1828 in Brunswick, Virginia, and Dr. Reed Haskins who was a member of the House of Delegates. Haskins' enslaved camp cook, known as Uncle Jimmy Matthews, so the story says, trapped some squirrels and prepared a thick stew with onions and stale bread, which awaited Haskins and his fellow hunters back at their campsite. Though they were at first shy to try the concoction when they learned of its ingredients, the men came to love it. Rumor has it that Matthews was tasked with recreating his stew for President Andrew Jackson at a political rally.

2 squirrels	2 onions, sliced
2 rabbits	½ cup celery leaves
1 pint canned tomatoes, diced	1 stick butter
6 ears corn, kernels cut from the cob	¼ cup sugar
2 cups fresh lima beans	Salt and black pepper to taste
2 cups okra, chopped	¼ cup cider vinegar
2 potatoes, sliced	2 tablespoons ketchup

Put cleaned squirrels and rabbits in a large pot with enough water to cover. Simmer 4 hours until meat is tender and pulls away from bones. Remove meat from broth and debone. Add the vegetables to the prepared broth followed by the butter, sugar, salt, pepper, vinegar, and ketchup. Simmer until thick. Add the meat back to the broth and cook for 5 minutes longer. Serve hot.

SOUTHERN SLANG

Phila often wrote cute quips of southern slang to accompany her Appalachian recipes, printing the below in several of her cookbooks including the official cookbook of the 1982 World's Fair, *600 International & Appalachian • Southern Recipes.*

They's stews an' stews, honey, but ter my min' th' ain't nothin' so satisfyin' as ol' time brunswick stew. Some folks holts that Brunswick stew air gotta be made outer squir'l but they's others what thinks nothin' cyarn't beat chicken. Since we got a chicken kilt an' picked an' cut up ready an' the squir'ls air still a hoppin' from limb ter limb in the parkI reckon we'll take chicken this time an' save the squir'l rule till campin' out time. Salt an' pepper yo' j'inted chicken an' roll it in flour. Now cut up a half poun'er salt po'k inter a hot skillet an' drap yo' chicken in an' brown it slow an' keerful long with po'k. Slice up two good sized onions an' fry 'em in the shillet with chicken an' chicken fixin's. Now scrape out all the contempts er the skillet inter yo' big 'lulimum pot. Kiver it with 'bout a quart er water. Open up a big can er termattersies an' dump it in. If you air so sitchumated you kin git fraish vegtables so much better but Brunswick stew made outter canned things ain't ter say nasty. Now a can er butterbeans, one er' okry an' three good sized Irish 'taters peeled an' cut cut up fineish. Ain't it got no cawn in it? Yes, honey, but too much cookin' makes cawn hard an' I never puts it in the pot till 'bout five minutes befo' sarvin'. Now throw in a han'ful er rice an' season keerful. That's where the gumption comes in. When the stew comes ter a good bubblin' bile turn yo' fire down real low an' go off an' fergit it. Brunswick stew oughter be good an' thickish. When the time comes ter sarve it an' you done added the can er cawn, or the fraish cawn as the case may be, if it air too juicy like, you kin thicken the mess either with flour or with a iron spoon er cooked oatmeal. I favors col' oatmeal as a thickenin'. It air smooth an' somehow don't tas'e so starchy. On the days you have this here stew 'tain't wuth while ter cook up no mo' victuals. It air a meal in itself.

SMOKED GOAT MULLIGATAWNY

MAKES 12 SERVINGS

A QUALITY GOAT LEG IS IMPORTANT FOR THIS DISH! Go to your local farmers' market and look for those who raise sheep and goats. *Buy local.* A baby goat leg weighs around 3 to 4 pounds. Pulling at the same nostalgic heartstrings as chicken and dumplings or grits, this dish makes my nostrils flare due to memories of my time in Kochi, India, at its spice markets with all of their smells and feels. If you'd like to make this as a vegetarian dish (and save a lot of time), simply make the soup and skip the goat.

FOR THE GOAT:

6 large garlic cloves, minced

5 tablespoons tarragon, finely chopped

4 anchovies, finely chopped

1 tablespoon cayenne pepper seeds

2 tablespoons salt

¼ cup brown sugar

1 tablespoon cumin powder

½ cup yellow mustard

1 quart plus ¼ cup cheap whiskey, divided

2 lemons, halved and squeezed

1 whole bone-in goat leg, about 5 pounds

½ cup coriander seeds, roasted

5 pounds apple wood chips

12 sprigs rosemary

20 pounds split white oak

FOR THE SOUP:

2 tablespoons butter

2 medium yellow onions, chopped

6 garlic cloves, minced

4 teaspoons fresh ginger, grated

4 teaspoons vindaloo curry (if this is too spicy, use madras)

2 teaspoons turmeric

2 teaspoons garam masala

8 cups chicken broth

2 pounds Okinawa sweet potatoes, peeled and diced

4 firm Concorde pears, peeled and diced

1 smoked goat leg, meat pulled from the bone

3⅓ cups coconut milk

2 cups heavy cream

Salt and pepper, to taste

1 ½ cups unsweetened coconut flakes, toasted

2 cups cilantro leaves, loosely chopped

Steamed rice for serving

(continued on next page)

SMOKED GOAT MULLIGATAWNY

(continued from previous page)

PREPARE THE GOAT: Combine the garlic, tarragon, anchovies, pepper seeds, salt, brown sugar, cumin, mustard, and ¼ cup whiskey in a mixing bowl, then add the lemon juice. Divide mixture in half. Use a sharp knife to make diagonal slits across both sides of the goat leg, being careful not to puncture the meat. Generously coat the leg in half of the marinade, massaging it into the slits to reinforce the flavor. Firmly pat the leg with the roasted coriander seeds, pressing them in on all of sides. Cover and refrigerate for 6 to 8 hours.

Soak apple wood chips and rosemary in 1 quart whiskey. In cauldron or pit, fire up one third of the white oak and let it burn until grey in color. Break wood up into medium-sized chunks. Place leg onto a smoker's grate. Add prepared, burning white oak chunks under grate and top embers with one third of the whiskey-soaked wood chips and rosemary. Close the smoker, leaving the vent just barely open. Start more white oak the same way as before, replenishing the smoker with fresh embers and a little more whiskey-soaked wood chips and rosemary every hour until goat is done, 6 to 8 hours (internal temperature of leg should be 145 degrees). With a small mop head or brush, baste the leg with reserved marinade every other hour.

MAKE THE SOUP: In a large pot, melt the butter and sauté onions until lightly browned. Add the garlic, ginger, and spices, and sauté for 1 more minute. Add the chicken broth, stirring to scrape up any stuck bits. Add the sweet potatoes, cover, and bring to a boil. Once boiling, uncover and reduce heat to a simmer, cooking for about 8 more minutes or until potatoes are tender. Add diced pears and goat, then simmer 5 more minutes. Stir in the coconut milk and cream with a rubber spatula, folding to evenly incorporate everything. Season with salt and pepper if desired. Simmer 20 to 30 more minutes, stirring occasionally. Ladle into bowls and garnish with toasted coconut and cilantro. Serve over rice.

SOW GOOD SLAW

MAKES 8 SERVINGS

THERE IS NOT MUCH TO EXPLAINING SLAW. If you know, you know, as the saying goes. Though, there is slaw, and there is coleslaw. I'm in the minority that detests the creamy side dish made popular by fast food conglomerates. Yes, coleslaw can be great! It can be delicious, in fact. But I love SLAW! My love affair with kohlrabi began while I was staging at the Old School Farm-To-Table Restaurant. I adapted Phila's recipe to create this ultimate sandwich topper.

1 cup white vinegar

¾ cup salad oil

2 teaspoons sugar, plus ⅞ cup

2 teaspoons salt

1 teaspoon dry mustard

1 teaspoon celery seed

1 teaspoon dill weed

1 teaspoon white pepper

½ teaspoon cayenne

1 medium head cabbage, shredded

1 medium onion, sliced thin

1 large carrot, shredded

2 bulbs purple kohlrabi, spiralized

In a saucepan, combine vinegar, oil, 2 teaspoons sugar, salt, mustard, celery seed, dill, white pepper, and cayenne, and bring to a boil. In a large bowl, alternate layers of cabbage, onion, carrot, and kohlrabi. Top vegetables with remaining sugar. Pour hot mixture over vegetables. Cover and let stand for 4 to 6 hours. Toss well before serving. Reserved in an air-tight container, this will keep, refrigerated, for 2 to 3 weeks.

Sow Good Slaw pictured on page 120.

HACHLAND CAESAR

SERVES 10

CAESAR SALAD IS, IN MY OPINION, one of the most unique tastes for a first course. Kale caesar became a newfound love for me when my father took me to one of his real estate client's new restaurant openings to introduce me to his favorite salad. Adele's, a Jonathan Waxman restaurant, has since become a Nashville favorite. At first, I thought, "Great, more kale…just trying to appease the transplants." Contrary to my original opinion, I now believe that kale caesar salads are one of the few recipe adaptations that is better than its founding classic. The Hachland Caesar is now my father's favorite, but, he tells me, Adele's is still a close second.

12 anchovy fillets packed in oil, drained

2 small garlic cloves

Kosher salt, plus more to taste

4 egg yolks

4 tablespoons fresh lemon juice

1 ½ teaspoons Dijon mustard

2 tablespoons barrel-aged red wine vinegar

4 tablespoons olive oil, plus more to toss with cornbread

1 cup vegetable oil

1 cup parmesan cheese, plus more for garnish

Pepper to taste

3 bunches kale (I like a mix of lacinato, green curly, and red russian kale)

1 pan of cornbread, dried overnight in the pan

Red pepper flakes (optional)

Lemon gem marigolds for garnish (optional)

Preheat oven to 350 degrees.

Rinse anchovy fillets and pat dry with paper towels. In a food processor, combine anchovy with garlic and two pinches of salt. Pulse until paste forms. Scrape down the sides with a spatula a few times to fully incorporate. Add the egg yolks, lemon juice, mustard, and vinegar and blend to combine. Gradually pour the olive oil through the top of the processor, followed by the vegetable oil. Puree until dressing is thick and glossy. Add parmesan and pulse. Season with salt and pepper.

Wash kale leaves with cold water and pat dry with paper towels. Strip leaves from stem and chop into small pieces.

Dice cornbread. Toss in a bowl with olive oil, salt, and pepper. Place on a baking sheet and bake for about 20 minutes, shuffling the croutons once or twice during the baking process.

In a large bowl, fold the caesar dressing into the kale until it is evenly incorporated. Plate a handful in the center of each plate and top with croutons and more parmesan. Sprinkle with crushed pepper, and garnish with lemon gem marigolds, if using.

STUFFED PEARS *with* LORENZO DRESSING

SERVES 4

PHILA CREATED THIS DISH, defined by its sweet and spicy contrast, for a unique starter course at her banquet dinners in the ballroom of Hachland Hill in Clarksville. I actually don't recall ever eating it as a child—but that may have been a testament to a child's unwillingness to try something unusual. (I'm sure she offered it to a stubborn younger me.) I caught a wild hare in recent years, eager to try some recipes of hers that I passed on in my youth, and made this dish, which turned out to be tremendously satisfying. I subbed Huy Fong Foods chili garlic sauce in lieu of the milder, unspecified chili sauce that she used in her original recipe. The increased spice content perfectly complements the creamy comfort of the blue cheese. I later made some pear-juice marinated fried chicken and drizzled it with the dressing, which is also a fantastic treat. I wish I could go back and eat every interesting food that I refused as little boy at her table!

FOR THE PEARS:

4 whole ripe pears

4 tablespoons blue or Roquefort cheese, room temperature

Watercress leaves

FOR THE LORENZO DRESSING:

¼ cup white vinegar

2 teaspoons salt

½ teaspoon English mustard

1 garlic clove, minced

2 teaspoons Worcestershire sauce

¾ cup vegetable oil

Dash fresh cracked pepper

Dash Tabasco sauce

⅓ cup Huy Fong Foods chili garlic sauce

PREP THE PEARS: Peel pears, leaving stem on. Core out center from bottom and fill the cavity with preferred cheese. Place in refrigerator and chill.

MAKE THE DRESSING: Mix first 8 ingredients together in a food processor and puree until smooth. Add chili sauce and pulse to combine. Stir well just before serving.

TO SERVE: Place pears on a bed of watercress and drizzle with Lorenzo dressing.

WILD GREENS *and* NASTURTIUM SALAD *with* PHILAMOT DRESSING

MAKES 5 SERVINGS

GROWING UP, WHENEVER WE'D HAVE A SLUMBER PARTY AT HACHLAND HILL, there was only one dressing or sauce that mattered to us children and our friends. Phila created a yellow, curry-based thick sauce that went with any and all foods. One of her former live-in guests used to swear by the fact that she'd eat it on ice cream. (It was good stuff, but that comment used to jar my stomach. In fact, it still does. But maybe don't knock curried vanilla ice cream until you try it.) Anyway, my brother deemed this product Phifee's Magic.

She never wrote the recipe down in its entirety, but printed hundreds of "Phifee's Magic Recipe Cards" only listing eggs, oil, garlic, yellow curry, and black pepper. That was Phila. I remember that her original recipe called for Sprite among many other ingredients. I made it with her when I was very, very little more than once, but I unfortunately cannot remember that far back in time to rustle up the ingredients from memory.

Once I was in high school, she would take creative liberties with whatever contraband was confiscated when I'd have a party at Hachland Hill. Natural Light was no fitting substitution for Sprite in this recipe, or probably any recipe for that matter, but she made it with no qualms. We could taste our Saturday night spoils in her "contraband cooking" the next day. Fast forward to today, and I make something that hits the taste buds just like Phifee's Magic. This one doesn't have curry or the bright yellow color that made hers so recognizable. And, I wasn't trying to recreate her magic. But still, this one hits home like no other sauce I've made at Hachland Hill. It is our new house dressing, and we call it Philamot on our menus.

FOR THE PHILAMOT DRESSING:

3 large garlic cloves

1 cup dried bergamot

2 egg yolks

¾ cup Dijon mustard

Zest of 2 Meyer lemons

Juice of 1 Meyer lemon

1 tablespoon Maggi seasoning

¼ cup Pommery barrel-aged red wine vinegar

2 tablespoons sugar

¼ cup olive oil

1 cup Sprite

2 cups vegetable oil

1 tablespoon black pepper

¼ cup honey

4 pinches salt

FOR THE SALAD:

4 cups mixed wild tender greens, chopped (I use a selection of dandelion, lamb's quarter, sorrel, chickweed, and purslane)

3 ramps, chopped

8 nasturtium flowers

3 tablespoons hot bacon drippings

Juice of 1 lemon

Philamot dressing

2-3 watermelon radishes, shaved, for garnish

Toasted pumpkin seeds for garnish

Crumbled feta cheese for garnish (optional)

MAKE THE DRESSING: Combine garlic and bergamot in a food processor and puree until a light paste forms. Add the yolks, mustard, lemon zest and juice, Maggi, vinegar, and sugar, then blend until evenly incorporated. Add the olive oil and Sprite and pulse to combine. While blending, slowly pour in the vegetable oil through the top of the food processor. Add the black pepper, honey and salt, and blend until smooth.

MAKE THE SALAD: Combine all salad ingredients in a bowl and toss to evenly coat with the bacon grease and lemon juice. Divide salad between 5 plates and drizzle dressing over top. Garnish with shaved watermelon radish and toasted pumpkin seeds. Sprinkle with crumbled feta if desired.

GRILLED WEDGE

MAKES 6 SERVINGS

I'VE ALWAYS LOVED A CLASSIC WEDGE. And then, there was a renaissance of cabbage—it started to find its way onto menus everywhere. So, I adapted my former recipe, which called for red gem lettuce heads, and the result was delicious. This became a very popular recipe during our virtual couple's cooking classes, which we hosted during the Covid-19 pandemic. If you don't find sweetness in the spiciness of life, this dressing and its walnuts are not for you.

1 large head cabbage, red or purple

⅔ cup olive oil, plus 2 tablespoons

Salt and pepper

4 tablespoons cayenne pepper

1 tablespoon garlic powder

1 tablespoon dill weed

1 tablespoon celery seed

2 tablespoons light brown sugar

2 cups raw walnuts

Roquefort dressing (page 231)

1 cup strawberries, sliced

Preheat oven to 350 degrees. Heat a grill.

Cut the head of cabbage in half, then cut each half into thirds vertically to keep them intact; you should have a total of 6 wedges. Lightly rub the wedges all over with the 2 tablespoons of olive oil and sprinkle with salt and pepper. Place the wedges on the grill grate over high flames for a 1 to 2 minutes per side until charred. Remove and let cool.

Combine the cayenne, ⅔ cup olive oil, garlic powder, 1 teaspoon salt, dill weed, celery seed, and brown sugar in a bowl and whisk vigorously until fully incorporated. Toss walnuts in the oil mixture and place them on a sheet tray lined with parchment paper. Bake for 12 minutes. Remove from oven and let cool. Crush up the walnuts, leaving some whole, but creating some fine crumbs. Place one grilled cabbage wedge on each plate. Drizzle Roquefort dressing over the wedge, garnish with sliced strawberries, and sprinkle walnut mixture over top.

TENNESSEE CAPRESE

MAKES 12 SERVINGS

FRIED GREEN TOMATOES were always an afterthought to me as a child. They were on the table at a lot of family-style suppers, but I didn't pay them much mind. Fifteen years later and suddenly, there they were popping up on hip gastropub and fine-dining menus everywhere I looked. Fried green tomatoes are cool now. Couples often want a menu that appeals to the crowd, with familiar favorites, but also want to reflect their venue, too. This is why I came up with our wedding reception cocktail-hour staple, the Tennessee Caprese. It is our take on a classic caprese with a nod to the South.

8 large green tomatoes, cored and sliced ½-inch thick

2 tablespoons Lowry's seasoning

1 tablespoon black pepper

1 quart buttermilk

2 cups yellow cornmeal

½ cup all-purpose flour

1 teaspoon smoked paprika

1 teaspoon garlic powder

½ teaspoon cayenne pepper

Kosher salt, to taste

4 large eggs

4 cups bacon grease or vegetable oil

2 pounds fresh mozzarella, sliced

Balsamic fig reduction (recipe follows)

Fresh basil, chiffonade

Place the tomato slices in a bowl and add the Lowry's and black pepper. Massage them so that the tomatoes are evenly coated in seasoning. Pour the buttermilk over the tomatoes until they are completely submerged. Cover and refrigerate overnight.

(continued on next page)

(continued from previous page)

The next day, combine the meal, flour, paprika, garlic powder, cayenne, and salt in a shallow bowl. Lightly beat the eggs in another bowl. Strain the tomatoes and pat dry. Heat oil in a heavy skillet over medium-high heat. Line a tray or baking sheet with paper towels.

Dip each tomato slice in the beaten eggs, and shake slightly to remove excess. Dredge slices in the dry mix and shake off excess meal. In batches of 4 or 5 (or however many your skillet allows) carefully drop the tomatoes into the hot oil. Fry until golden brown, flipping once, about 2 to 3 minutes per side. Transfer to paper towel-lined tray to absorb the grease. Repeat with remaining batches. Serve topped with sliced mozzarella, drizzled with balsamic fig reduction, and garnished with basil.

BALSAMIC FIG REDUCTION

MAKES 1 CUP

2 tablespoons melted butter

2 shallots, diced

1 cup balsamic vinegar

2 sprigs thyme

¾ cup fig preserves

Heat butter in a small saucepan over medium heat. Add shallots and cook for 2 minutes. Add the vinegar and thyme and bring to a low boil, whisking until sauce has reduced by a third and is thick and syrupy. Add the fig preserves and simmer, whisking constantly to evenly incorporate. Add a shot of water if it becomes too thick.

EGG SALAD TOAST

SERVES 8

EGG SALAD: That Southern market, grab n' go and picnic favorite. I'm embarrassed to admit that I had never tried a bite of egg salad until 2020, when I was recruited to help with the revival of Nashville's iconic Elliston Place Soda Shop. It was during the recipe research and development for the menu when we were working with recipes from the restaurant's chef as well as one from Randy Rayburn's arsenal. The soda shop had a history of being frequented by old timers so its recipes couldn't be too adventurous or spicy. The goal was to recreate the restaurant's original menu with fresh recipes. While it wasn't the right fit for the soda shop, I fell in love with the idea of truffle-infused egg salad, which came from one of Rayburn's late chefs at the former Sunset Grill. I adapted it into a dish that's now served at Hachland Hill, and it rounds out a picnic basket like nothing else.

12 hard-boiled eggs, peeled and chilled

¾ cup mayonnaise

1 tablespoon truffle oil

1 tablespoon Pommery Moutarde De Meaux french mustard

½ teaspoon white pepper

½ teaspoon salt

¼ teaspoon fenugreek

¼ teaspoon smoked paprika

1 tablespoon finely chopped dill

¼ cup diced celery

2 tablespoons chopped scallion

Brioche dough (page 174)*

Garlic butter

Microgreens and black Hawaiian fine grain finishing sea salt, for garnish

*NOTE: Fresh Market has great sliced brioche loaves if you want to save a step, or ask your favorite local bakery.

(continued on next page)

EGG SALAD TOAST

(continued from previous page)

Preheat oven to 350 degrees. Cut eggs in half and remove yolks to a bowl. With a whisk, crush the yolks by pressing down on them. Add the mayonnaise, truffle oil, mustard, and herbs, then whisk until smooth. Dice the reserved egg whites into small pieces. Fold the egg whites, dill, celery, and scallions into the yolk mixture until evenly distributed. Place in an airtight container and let chill for at least 1 hour or until ready to serve.

Shape Brioche dough into a loaf and place it into a greased bread mold. It should be about half the height of your pan. Proof for about 1 hour at 78 to 80 degrees, or covered at room temperature, until it's doubled in size and climbs to the top of the pan. Bake for 15 minutes or until top is nicely browned. Remove from oven and let cool.

Slice the cooled loaf into ¾-inch pieces. Brush with garlic butter and place in oven for 8 minutes. Flip the bread slices and continue to bake for 10 more minutes until a golden-brown crust has formed. Remove from oven and let the slices come to room temperature.

Spoon egg salad onto toasted bread and spread it evenly to cover the slice up to the crust. Garnish with microgreens and sprinkle with black Hawaiian fine grain finishing sea salt.

FIRE & ICE SUMMER SALAD

MAKES 10 SERVINGS

THOUGH IT'S A COMMON PICNIC SIDE OR STAPLE on many a lazy susan during the summer, I didn't create my own recipe for this salad until July 2020 as a result of the pandemic. When all of our spring events were canceled on account of Covid, I started a family-sized meal delivery service. A mason jar of Fire & Ice was one of the most popular orders during those heated summer months. Using locally sourced, fresh summer ingredients is what will make this a showstopper for your Fourth of July picnic.

½ cup apple cider vinegar

½ cup red wine vinegar

½ cup granulated sugar

2 teaspoons salt

2 teaspoons prepared horseradish

2 teaspoons celery seed

2 teaspoons mustard seed

2 medium green bell peppers, cut into thin strips

2 small red onions, halved and sliced thin

2 jalapeños, seeded and diced fine

6 large tomatoes, cut into chunks

4 medium cucumbers, peeled and sliced thin

¼ cup lovage leaves, chopped fine

2 tablespoons lemon verbena leaves, chopped fine

Combine the vinegars, sugar, salt, horseradish, celery seeds, and mustard seeds in a saucepan over medium heat. Stir and bring to a boil for 1 minute, then set aside. Combine the bell pepper, onion, jalapeños, and tomato in a large glass bowl so that they are evenly dispersed. Pour the hot vinegar mixture over the vegetables and set aside until cool. Add the cucumbers, lovage, and lemon verbena, then fold everything together with a rubber spatula to evenly incorporate. Cover with plastic wrap and refrigerate for at least 6 hours, or overnight. Serve with a slotted spoon to strain off excess liquid.

Chapter 3

———

MEATS & ACCOMPANIMENTS

———

Phila's Story

PART 3

PHILA, HOMING IN ON HER PASSION FOR WRITING by learning and sharing recipes from different regions of the world, added more cookbooks to her resume. She published *From Phila with Love, Hachland Hill Recipes: Nashville's Famous Caterer Shares her Secrets* in 1973 and *Kountry Kooking* in 1974. Given her celebrity status on account of her television show and books, she was asked by former U.S. Senator Howard Baker to prepare a special Tennessee luncheon for the historic United Nations visit to Nashville in 1976. This was the first meeting ever for the United Nations away from New York City.

The luncheon was held at Nashville's Centennial Park for 1,800 dignitaries from around the world. "We didn't have a budget worth a penny but using what you have and making something out of nothing was my business," Phila said. "It was country cooking for the world."

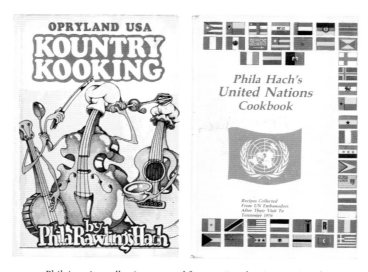

Phila's recipe collections ranged from regional to international.

Phila shared recipes and techniques to teach others to love cooking as she did.

Sponsors of her former cooking show donated meats and dairy products. A pilot, with whom she had flown in her flight attendant days, flew the ambassadors to Nashville free of charge. She was adamant that mint juleps be served for a proper presentation of the South, and Nashville Mayor Richard Fulton was equally adamant that they not be served due to conflicting liquor laws at the time. This was a hassle for her, but an experience she was eager to trump nonetheless. Phila oversaw Tennessee State Troopers' smuggling of Jack Daniels Black Label whiskey, disguised in Purity milk cartons, from the distillery in Lynchburg, Tennessee, to the Coca-Cola bottling plant in Clarksville, where she mixed the juleps in the dark of night.

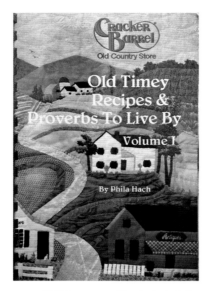 

Phila's many cookbooks included numerous collections for Cracker Barrel.

She told me all about the impressive catering feat, how she served country ham and other Southern delicacies to former Secretary of State Henry Kissinger as well as countless other notable names. Someone once asked her if Kissinger ate the ham, to which she responded, "Honey, there were Muslims there who ate the ham." What began with scavenging for money proved to be a tremendous outcome, commemorated by the

"We didn't have a budget worth a penny but using what you have and making something out of nothing was my business," Phila said. "It was country cooking for the world."

Historical Commission of Metropolitan Nashville and Davidson County with a waymark that now sits in Centennial Park. She published *Phila Hach's United Nations Cookbook* in 1981.

In the winter of 1981, Phila visited Knoxville as the city prepared to host the 1982 World's Fair that would take place from May to October. The Sunsphere, the symbol of that year's fair, towered over the city. There was a full-service restaurant and observation deck at its top during the fair. (The

Sunsphere closed shortly after the end of the fair.) When they announced the event, Phila's son Joe suggested that she reach out to Beau Roberts, who was heading up the occasion, to see if she could write a cookbook for it. The conversation resulted in a resounding yes from everyone involved. She published *600 International & Appalachian • Southern Recipes, the Official Cookbook for the 1982 World's Fair in Knoxville, Tennessee*, which was comprised of recipes she selected, compiled, and edited herself. Its content came from her previous cookbooks, *Kitchen Kollege, From Phila with Love, Kountry Kooking,* and *The United Nations Cookbook.* Cracker Barrel carried the cookbook, and its successful sales delivered another knocking opportunity to her always "open door."

Danny Evins, the founder of Cracker Barrel, contacted her with a proposal that would steer her career into the nineties. Evins explained that Cracker Barrel had never manufactured a logotype item, so he sought Phila's authorship for his company's first trademarked cookbook. *Cracker Barrel Old Country Stores: Old Fashion Intentions* was printed in 1983, and she wrote three more for them: *Old Timey Recipes and Proverbs to Live By (Cracker Barrel Old Country Store Vol I)* printed in that same year; *American Holidays Cookbook (Cracker Barrel Old Country Store Vol II)* in 1985; and *Recipes and Health Secrets to Make You Live Longer (Cracker Barrel Old Country Store Vol III)* in 1990.

Phila enjoying a view of Knoxville's Sunsphere

FRIED CHICKEN

SERVES 4

WHEN MISS RUTH TAUGHT ME HOW TO MAKE HACHLAND HILL FRIED CHICKEN, she showed me how she soaked the chicken quickly in hot water before dredging it. I just assumed that was the norm for frying chicken. The hot water relaxes the meat and seals in the juices, while also allowing more flour to stick to the chicken. This gives our fried chicken a special crispy character. Years later, while working with the team behind the revival of Nashville's iconic Elliston Place Soda Shop, I delved deep into the subject of fried chicken on account of the restaurant being a meat & three. Lynn Chandler, who founded the soda shop in 1939, actually coined the concept of a meat & three. Southern comfort food, particularly at cafeteria-style establishments, is commonly offered in servings defined by the quantity of proteins or side vegetables on the plate. You can order a meat & one, meat & two, meat & three, or all sides for the vegetarians. (But be warned: The sides cooked without any hock or trimmings are slim pickings at a real meat & three!)

During our fried chicken talks, much to my surprise, I learned that no one else used the hot-water method. One day while sitting at Midtown Café with our crew, I mentioned that Phila always claimed that the popular Nashville restaurant Monell's, known for its comfort food, used her fried chicken recipe. (I've said it before and I'll say it again, my grandma was known to stretch the truth. I had no idea if the claim was real or a tall tale.) Well, one of the members of the soda shop project called up the owner of Monell's right then and there. Sure enough, they dabble with hot water, too, they said. They clearly have made the recipe their own with some adaptations, but Phila laid the groundwork. I've made my own adaptation to her recipe here by adding what I like to call "Marvel Dust."

3 cups plus 2 tablespoons
   all-purpose flour

Lowry's seasoned salt

Black pepper

Lard or oil

1 large chicken, cut into 8 pieces,
   at room temperature

Marvel Dust (optional, recipe
   follows)

1 cup cream

Salt

(continued on next page)

FRIED CHICKEN

(continued from previous page)

Sift together 3 cups flour, salt, and pepper to taste in a deep dish or bowl. Set a deep, heavy skillet over medium-low heat and fill it with ½ to ¾ inches of lard or oil. Fill a large bowl with hot tap water and set beside flour. (Water should be as hot as your sink allows; no need to boil it.)

Working in batches of 2 or 3 pieces, submerge chicken in bowl of hot water for 15 to 20 seconds, then immediately coat with the seasoned flour and quickly place in the skillet skin side down. Cover the skillet and fry for 5 to 8 minutes. (Note: Cooking time will vary depending on the size of the cuts.) Remove cover and cook for 4 to 8 minutes. Turn the chicken and cover for 5 to 8 more minutes. Remove cover and cook 4 to 8 more minutes. By now the chicken should be brown, crunchy, and cooked through. Set pieces on a rack to cool and sprinkle with Marvel Dust, if using. Repeat with remaining batches.

To make pan gravy, pour all but 2 tablespoons of fat from the pan. Add 2 tablespoons flour and stir until blended. Add ½ cup hot water and 1 cup cream. Stir and cook until gravy is thick. Season with salt and pepper to taste.

MARVEL DUST

1 packet dry ranch seasoning

¼ teaspoon smoked paprika

**1 teaspoon distilled white
   vinegar powder**

Combine all ingredients in a bowl and stir to combine. Store in an airtight container at room temperature.

WEST GERMAN CHICKEN

SERVES 8

I REMEMBER EATING SOMETHING SIMILAR TO THIS DISH as a child visiting Hachland Hill on the weekends. I used to call all breaded chicken "flat chicken." There was no rhyme or reason to the nickname, but it stuck with me. I found this recipe in one of Phila's cookbooks much later in life and loved it for two reasons. One, it brought me back to the flat chicken of yesteryear. And two, it was a German-inspired recipe, and apparently one of my grandfather's favorite dishes that Phila made. I never got to meet my grandfather, who was known as Papa, but I feel something special when cooking and tasting recipes that I know he favored.

FOR THE CHICKEN:

2 whole fryer chickens

2 egg yolks, divided

Breadcrumbs

Parmesan cheese

¼ cup frying oil or fat

FOR THE SAUCE:

4 tablespoons butter

4 tablespoons flour

2 cups milk

½ cup chopped mushrooms

1 carrot, sliced and boiled until tender

1 onion, boiled until tender

Bouquet of herbs

½ cup cooking sherry

2 egg yolks

Cut each chicken into 8 pieces. Stir together 2 egg yolks in one shallow bowl. In another shallow bowl, combine breadcrumbs and parmesan. Dip each piece of chicken in egg yolk, then breadcrumb mixture. In a large skillet, heat oil over medium heat. In batches, sauté chicken pieces until brown and tender.

Make a white sauce by adding flour, butter, and milk to a saucepan and stirring over medium heat until combined. Add mushrooms, carrot, onion, and herbs, and stir to combine. Add the sherry and beaten egg yolks just before serving. Serve chicken with sauce.

TENNESSEE COUNTRY HAM

SERVES 12

(with leftovers for biscuits the next morning!)

QUALITY IS KEY WITH COUNTRY HAM. Choose one that is at least 18 months old—we typically like a 2-year ham. My dad has always been in charge of the hams at our holidays, and I won't try to take that from him as long as he is willing to take it on. He makes one that "will make you want to smack your children," as he always says of anything downright tasty. To me, there is no taste like a properly prepared country ham.

1 bone-in country ham	½ cup brown sugar
½ cup cornmeal	Beaten biscuits (page 53)

Soak whole ham overnight in cool water. The next day, saw off the hock end.

Preheat oven to 300 degrees. Place ham in a deep pan and fill with warm water until ham is almost covered. Place ham in oven and cook, allowing for 20 minutes per pound. (An 18-pound ham will take about 6 hours).

Pull ham from oven and remove skin while it's still hot. Increase oven temperature to 450 degrees. Combine cornmeal and brown sugar. Pat mixture all over the top of the skinned ham. Place back into oven and cook until the top of the ham is browned.

Remove from oven and let cool to room temperature. Once cool, refrigerate until ready to serve. To serve, slice thin and serve with beaten biscuits.

BEEF TENDERLOIN *with* GARLIC CHIVE HORSERADISH SAUCE

SERVES 10

I KNOW EXACTLY WHICH TWO RECIPES I FIRST MADE WITH PHILA. Chocolate nut drop cookies and apple crepes with vanilla-bourbon sauce. Something about cracking eggs and dough-covered fingers were great fun for me as a child. Savory applications with her came a little later in life; maybe because with meat comes knives and butchery, which both require a little more maturity and steadier hands. Beef tenderloin and leg of lamb were the first two cuts of meats that we tackled together. Her tenderloin was a family favorite and a staple at Hachland Hill. It still is today. She would make it for every family holiday, along with her rolls and twice-baked potatoes. Those three things are a match made in heaven. She would only do salt and pepper with her tenderloin, that was it, and it was simplicity at its finest. I now use locally sourced beef for the iconic dish at Hachland Hill, and I prepare it with just a slight variation of her recipe. My brother, who always regarded her tenderloin and potatoes as his favorite meal, admitted to favoring my tenderloin at the holidays since her passing. I had a good teacher.

FOR THE BEEF:

1 (4-5 pound) whole beef
    tenderloin

Salt

Pepper

Garlic powder

1 tablespoon Maggi seasoning

FOR THE HORSERADISH SAUCE:

2 cups mayonnaise

¼ cup sour cream

½ cup garlic chives

2 small cloves garlic

Prepared horseradish to taste

1 teaspoon salt

1 teaspoon smoked paprika

Pea shoot tendrils to garnish

(continued on next page)

BEEF TENDERLOIN WITH
GARLIC CHIVE HORSERADISH SAUCE

(continued from previous page)

MAKE THE TENDERLOIN: Remove the chain and the silver skin from the tenderloin. (This can be done for you by a local butcher.) Tie tenderloin with butcher's twine so it is tight and uniform in size from end to end. Rub generously with salt and pepper, then sprinkle with garlic powder and rub that in as well. Let rest in the refrigerator overnight.

The next day, preheat the oven to 350 degrees and place tenderloin in a roasting rack set on a sheet tray. Sprinkle the Maggi evenly over top of the tenderloin. Roast in oven for about 45 minutes for medium rare.

MEANWHILE, MAKE THE SAUCE: Combine mayonnaise, sour cream, garlic chives, garlic, and prepared horseradish in a food processor. Pulse until smooth. Season with salt and smoked paprika.

Remove from the oven and let rest. Cut off the twine. Slice tenderloin to desired thickness. Serve with cream and garnish with pea shoot tendrils.

LEG OF LAMB

SERVES 10

LAMB IS QUITE POSSIBLY MY FAVORITE PROTEIN. It is also a memory of Phila. When I first started to really get into cooking, she would make the short trips from Hachland Hill to our family home in Nashville and teach me one dish. I remember standing in the kitchen on Vossland Drive with her, so giddy to be learning something new, and eager to pull the fruits of our labor from the oven. This recipe is one full of anticipation, because its aroma can waft throughout your whole neighborhood. This lamb goes great with Pepper Jelly-Glazed Carrots (page 149) and Mint Aïoli (page 230).

1 whole bone-in leg of lamb, trimmed

Sea salt

Black pepper

Garlic powder

3 carrots

6 red potatoes

3 quarts apple cider vinegar

Fresh rosemary

Fresh thyme

Fresh sage

6 garlic cloves

1 tablespoon cornstarch

Preheat oven to 325 degrees. Generously coat the lamb on all sides with salt, pepper, and garlic powder. Place in a deep pan. Cut off the tops of the carrots and cut all but a few of the potatoes in half. Arrange the carrots and potatoes around the lamb. Fill the pan with a 4-to-1 ratio of water to vinegar so that it reaches about halfway up the meat. Add the herbs and garlic to the liquid and place a few sprigs of each herb on top of the leg. Tent pan with foil.

Place pan in oven and roast for 4 hours. If the pan gets dry, add more of the water/vinegar (in ratio) as necessary.

Remove lamb from oven. Discard the herbs and garlic cloves. Reserve the potatoes and carrots to be served alongside. Remove lamb from pan and let rest. Pour juices into a saucepan and bring liquid to a boil. Combine cornstarch with 2 tablespoons water to make a slurry and add to the boiling au jus. Season to taste. To serve, slice or pull lamb and serve with au jus on the side.

TURKEY AND CORNBREAD DRESSING

SERVES 12

(plus leftovers for sleepy sandwiches the next day)

I ADMIT THAT I'VE ALWAYS BEEN SOMEWHAT OF AN ODD BIRD (pun intended) for the fact that, hold your breath, I don't love turkey. I look forward to the ham, oysters, duck, and so many other yummies at Thanksgiving before the star of the show. Once I took the helm at Hachland Hill, I immediately found myself tasked with catering holiday meals for large families staying at our Spring Creek Inn. My favorite way to serve the holiday birds are brined and smoked to perfection. I've experimented with other techniques as well, but something about Phila's no-frills approach to the gobbler hits just right. This is a bird that needs no introduction or special tricks, just a room filled with family to feed.

FOR THE TURKEY:

1 (10-15-pound) turkey

FOR THE CORNBREAD DRESSING:

4 cups cornbread, torn

2 cups leftover cold biscuits, torn

⅓ cup grated onion

1 cup grated celery

2 tablespoons chopped parsley

1 ½ teaspoons salt

1 teaspoon poultry seasoning

1 teaspoon sage

½ teaspoon pepper

Turkey broth from pan

4 heaping tablespoons melted butter

1 pint shucked oysters (optional)

FOR THE GRAVY:

Remaining broth from turkey pan

1 tablespoon cornstarch

Salt and pepper

Hard-boiled eggs, sliced (optional)

MAKE THE TURKEY: Preheat oven to 300 degrees. Wrap turkey in a well-greased muslin cloth. Place in large roasting pan with sufficient water to make gravy later, about 4 to 5 cups. Bake in oven, allowing 25 minutes per pound. Remove from oven and transfer turkey to a cutting board. Reserve broth for gravy and dressing.

MAKE THE CORNBREAD DRESSING: While turkey rests, increase oven to 375 degrees. Combine all ingredients in a large bowl, mixing thoroughly. Pour into a large baking dish and bake for 1 hour until brown. If dressing appears too dry, add hot water as it bakes and stir slightly to blend it in. If desired, 15 minutes before done, add oysters. Stir through dressing and allow to brown again.

MAKE THE GRAVY: Pour any remaining broth from the turkey pan into a saucepan. Heat over medium heat. Combine cornstarch with 2 tablespoons water and add slurry to the gravy. Season to taste with salt and black pepper. Add sliced eggs, if using. Serve turkey sliced with cornbread dressing and gravy on the side.

FRIED CATFISH

SERVES 8

THERE ISN'T ONE CHAPTER OF MY LIFE that doesn't include a catfish memory. It's the fish that keeps on giving! Way back before I could run a trotline, my dad would help me reel in catfish from the pond at Hachland Hill's farm, just for fun. A decade later, my brother and I would hike out to Marrowbone Lake, just through the woods from Hachland Hill, carrying our milk jugs and chicken livers. We had a lot of laughs on that water, and I know the country locals had their share of laughs at our expense—we'd roll up hot in our lacrosse pennies ready to drop some lines. But my taste for catfish was affirmed at a hunters' rejoice restaurant called Boyette's in Tiptonville, Tennessee, where our old duck club was located. The locals call it "Boyt's." They serve an all-you-can-eat catfish dinner. As a matter of fact, they have an all-you-can-eat dinner with the option to choose up to three proteins. In my last years of high school, when I was a heavyweight wrestler, I was keen on taking up that challenge, ordering catfish, fried chicken, and country ham steaks. The Hach boys about put them out of business! This is a go-to recipe and goes great with our Lemon-Lovage Tartar Sauce (page 232).

2 ½ cups yellow stone-ground cornmeal

1 cup all-purpose flour

1 teaspoon butter-flavored salt

3 teaspoons kosher salt

1 teaspoon garlic powder

¼ teaspoon white pepper

¼ teaspoon cayenne pepper

½ teaspoon dill weed

8 catfish filets

Milk

Frying oil

In a large bowl, sift together cornmeal, flour, and seasonings. Dip catfish filets in milk, letting any excess drip off, then dredge in the meal mixture and shake away clumps. Heat oil in a deep, heavy skillet until it reaches 365 degrees on a deep-fry thermometer. Add catfish filets in batches, frying until golden brown and flaky inside. Drain on paper towels and serve hot.

JOHNNY MOZETTEA

SERVES 10 TO 12

THIS DISH WAS CREATED BY TERESA MARZETTI in 1896 in Columbus, Ohio—her last name became the casserole's foundation, which my family calls "Mozettea." Johnny was Teresa's brother. She and her husband, Joseph, sought a simple and affordable main course, that would be particularly geared to the students of nearby Ohio State University. Named for her brother, the dish originally consisted of noodles, ground beef, cheese, and tomato sauce, and it was an immediate hit for 45 cents. Versions of it eventually surfaced in battlefield kitchens of the U.S. Army. It gained so much popularity with the troops in Panama that it spilled over into the local community. Panamanian culture influenced the addition of olives and Arturo sauce. Locals still call it Johnny Marzetti and claim it as their national dish.

My great grandmother, Sara Belle Bassett from my mom's side, was as good of a Southern cook as any, drawing on her tastes from a long-cultured life to bring home to her family and friends. We called her Gigi. She lived in Balboa, Panama, Canal Zone, from 1936 to 1941, before returning to Kentucky shortly before the outbreak of World War II. My grandmother, Betty June Bassett Clark, spoke often of her time in the Canal Zone where her father served with the Deputy United States Marshall. (My older brother, with his first-born birthright, gave a name to all of our grandparents. He called Betty June, BB.) Gigi brought her Johnny Mozettea recipe home with her, and it stuck.

Mary Lu Dempsey, women's editor for the *Kentucky New Era*, covered Gigi's life and recipes in her September 1972 article, "Varied Background of Recipes Makes Cooking Interesting."

Dempsey wrote: "'The first time I had ever eaten Johnny Mozettea was at a picnic in Panama on Ancon Hill. It was just so delightful that I was determined to have the recipe,' Mrs. Bassett said. After their return from Panama and moving into a home, Mrs. Bassett decided she wanted to entertain her friends at a luncheon. Even though the house itself was not finished and the stove wasn't connected, she invited guests for lunch."

The recipe traveled timelessly between the hands of my great grandmother and my mom's mom, BB, before mom made it her own. This was one of her nostalgic favorites, which she'd cook for our family during the holidays long after Gigi quit making it herself.

"It was passed down to BB," my mom said. "BB remembered so vividly and fondly her time living in Panama. It is so hearty, and flavorful. Serves a lot so good for a crowd. Add salad and bread, and you are all set."

2 pounds ground beef

1 pound onion, chopped

1 bunch celery, chopped

1 pound green peppers, chopped

1 can Arturo sauce*

1 can hot sauce

1 can tomato soup

1 can tomato paste

1 can mushrooms

2 packages spaghetti noodles

1 jar pimento stuffed green olives, sliced

1 pound sharp cheese, grated

*NOTE: You should be able to find this in the canned soup/sauce aisle.

Preheat oven to 325 degrees. Brown meat in a skillet over low heat, then add the onions, celery, and peppers. Add the sauces, soup, tomato paste, and mushrooms. Season to taste with salt and pepper. Boil noodles and drain well. Add noodles to the sauce and place in a casserole dish. Cover with cheese and olives. Bake for 1 hour or longer if needed.

BANH MEATLOAF

SERVES 8

"THERE WERE PEOPLE FROM AFRICA, THE MIDDLE EAST, ANYWHERE AND EVERYWHERE, and she always did a wonderful job and did wonderful things and had types of menus that were American but that also reflected the cuisines of the countries from where they were from," Brooks Parker, one of Phila's oldest friends and a former press secretary to a Tennessee governor, told me in an interview. This practice is still prevalent at Hachland Hill, especially in the wedding and retreat menus I create today, which are always tailored to each client. I love bridging cultures to create something special through food, something inherently Southern but inspired by another place. I'll never forget the time that I stumbled upon "Nashville Hot Chicken" at a hidden gem restaurant in Vietnam, which is where I developed my taste for banh mi and their thoughtfully placed ingredients. While I created this dish with the obvious play on words in mind, it is the beautiful and easy marriage between two different cuisines that makes recipes like this truly wonderful. This one is also great as a sandwich spread with sriracha mayo.

FOR THE GARNISH:

½ cup warm water

4 teaspoons sugar

2 teaspoons salt

½ cup rice vinegar

1 cup carrot, julienned

1 purple daikon, sliced thin

1 jalapeño, sliced thin

FOR THE MEATLOAF:

1 pound ground pork*

1 pound ground beef*

¼ cup fresh basil, finely chopped

3 scallions, finely chopped

2 garlic cloves, minced

1 teaspoon freshly ground pepper

1 teaspoon salt

2 teaspoons sugar

1 teaspoon Chinese five-spice powder

1 tablespoon fish sauce

1 tablespoon hot sauce (I prefer sriracha)

1 egg, beaten

6 tablespoons breadcrumbs (panko works well)

Cilantro sprigs

*NOTE: Be sure to choose a pork or beef with a good bit of marbling, and the second of the two can be a leaner grind.

(continued on next page)

BANH MEATLOAF

(continued from previous page)

MAKE THE GARNISH: To the warm water, add sugar and salt, then stir to dissolve. Stir in the vinegar. Set aside to cool. Add vegetables to the vinegar mixture. Set aside to marinate for at least 3 hours, stirring occasionally. Refrigerate if marinating for more than 3 hours.

MAKE THE MEATLOAF: Preheat oven to 375 degrees. Wrap a roasting rack with aluminum foil and poke holes in it with a paring knife or fork. Place the rack on a parchment-lined sheet tray. In a large bowl, loosely work the pork and beef together with wet hands. In a separate bowl, combine the basil, scallion, garlic, pepper, salt, sugar, and five spice. Add herb mixture to the ground meat, along with the fish sauce, hot sauce, egg, and breadcrumbs. Combine well with your hands but do not overwork it. Shape the meatloaf and place it on the foil-covered rack. Bake for 1 to 1½ hours, rotating it once halfway through cooking. Remove from the oven and let rest tented with foil. Slice meatloaf and top with pickled vegetables and cilantro sprigs.

FILET MIGNON

SERVES 2

I GREW UP EATING STEAK AT LEAST ONCE A WEEK, mostly at home on account of the lack of independent steakhouses in "Old Nashville." There were always a handful of finer dining options here and there throughout the city, but nothing like today with our now lavish buildouts and novel concepts opening up at every turn. Don't get me wrong: I love going out to eat and would be a liar if I said I didn't enjoy the finer things in life. But a lot of the restaurants from yesteryear that were responsible for pioneering Nashville's haute cuisine have been left in the dust by this new wave of epicurean establishments. Some have closed, and some that are still open are timeworn, to no fault of their own. My wife constantly jokes with me about the size and caliber of the steaks at a Hach family dinner—everything is over the top. This timeless recipe from Phila has brought me fond memories and an appreciation for the steakhouses of "Old Nashville," before classic cuts were topped with cotton candy and whatever else to stay current. It's not too big for my wife either, which is a win in my book.

FOR THE MARINADE AND STEAK:

½ cup vegetable oil

1 tablespoon lemon juice

3 teaspoons sugar

1 cup red wine

½ teaspoon salt

½ teaspoon cracked pepper

½ teaspoon dried herbs (I use
   marjoram and thyme)

2 (6-ounce) filet mignon*

1 tablespoon butter, melted

1 tablespoon oil

FOR THE BRANDY GLAZE:

¼ cup brandy

¼ cup water

2 tablespoons Worcestershire

*NOTE: I favor wagyu beef at Hachland Hill because who doesn't. The Fly Farm, south of Nashville, is Japanese certified and can be found at the Franklin Farmers Market.

(continued on next page)

FILET MIGNON

(continued from previous page)

Preheat oven to 450 degrees.

Combine all marinade ingredients except the meat in a bowl or shallow dish. Add filet mignon and let marinate for at least 1 hour. Place a heavy skillet over high heat and remove filets from marinade. Baste both sides in butter and oil. Sear in the skillet for 2 to 3 minutes per side.

While they sear, combine brandy glaze ingredients and drizzle over steaks, turning to coat both sides, then place the skillet directly into the preheated oven for a couple more minutes for rare to medium rare. Remove from oven and place filets on a cutting board to rest for a few minutes before serving.

POT ROAST *with* POTATO DUMPLINGS

SERVES 10

MY WIFE'S LOVE FOR HER GRANDMOTHER'S POT ROAST is what inspired me to research Phila's vast arsenal of recipes for this household favorite. I tested several of her printed versions and landed on this German-style approach, which my grandfather loved according to Phila's notes. An Instant Pot has expedited the process and made pot roast foolproof for many a home cook, but the old-fashioned method is a tried-and-true winner.

1 (5-pound) round steak or pot roast

1 tablespoon salt

½ teaspoon pepper

2 yellow onions, sliced

1 carrot, sliced

1 stalk celery, chopped

4 garlic cloves

4 peppercorns

1 pint red wine vinegar

2 bay leaves

2 tablespoons kidney fat or shortening

6 tablespoons butter (if meat is not too fatty)

5 tablespoons all-purpose flour

1 tablespoon sugar

8 gingersnaps, crushed

Potato dumplings (recipe follows)

Season roast with salt and pepper. Combine onions, carrots, celery, garlic, peppercorns, vinegar, and bay leaves and pour over meat in a pan or dish. Cover and let stand in refrigerator for 4 days.

(continued on next page)

POT ROAST WITH POTATO DUMPLINGS

(continued from previous page)

On the fifth day, drain the meat, reserving marinade liquid. Heat fat in a heavy-bottomed pan over medium-high heat and brown meat on all sides. Add marinade liquid and lower heat to medium. In a small saucepan, melt the butter, then add the flour and stir until smooth. Add the sugar and cook slowly until it tuns dark brown. Add butter mixture to the pan with the meat.

Simmer roast for about 4 hours until meat is done. Transfer meat from pan to a platter. Stir the crushed gingersnaps into the juices and cook until thick. Pour the sauce over the meat and potato dumplings.

POTATO DUMPLINGS

5 cups mashed potatoes

1 egg

1 teaspoon salt

¼ teaspoon white pepper

⅛ teaspoon nutmeg

1 cup all-purpose flour, plus more
   as needed

4 cups beef broth

Combine the potatoes, egg, salt, pepper, and nutmeg in a large bowl and mix thoroughly. Add enough flour to make a workable dough. Roll dough out into long ropes and cut off 1-inch pieces. Bring broth to a boil. Drop dumplings into broth, cover, and cook until dumplings are firm.

HOME COOK'S PULLED PORK

SERVES 10 TO 14

I'VE LONG BEEN FASCINATED WITH SMOKING MEATS. It's how we prepare our signature pulled pork, brisket, short ribs, chicken quarters, and even trout at Hachland Hill. Phila, on the other hand, was never much of a pitmaster herself. I grew up on her oven-braised pulled pork, which is fantastic. Countless crowds at company picnics and wedding receptions were blown away by her dish—and no one was able to tell it came from the oven unless she let them in on her process. I've added cloves and herbs to her recipe, and I will make it this way from time to time, especially if I am running low on sleep and the willpower to stay awake smoking through the night for an event. The liquid ratio can be tailored to your preference for more or less vinegary vigor.

1 bone-in Boston butt or shoulder

Kosher salt

Black pepper

¼ teaspoon cayenne pepper

½ teaspoon garlic powder

½ teaspoon mustard powder

8 garlic cloves

2 sprigs fresh sage

3 sprigs fresh dill

2 stalks fresh lovage

2-3 whole cloves

Mix of herbs (I use parsley and thyme)

Water

Apple cider vinegar

Preheat oven to 250 degrees. Generously coat the pork with salt and pepper on all sides. Rub the cayenne, garlic powder, and mustard powder onto the fat cap and sides. Place the pork into a deep pan and fill with a 2-to-1 ratio of water to vinegar, until it's about halfway up the sides of the meat. Add the garlic, sage, dill, and lovage to the liquid and place the cloves and mix of herbs on top of the meat. Place the pan in the oven, uncovered, and cook for 10 to 12 hours until the bone pulls easily from the meat. Remove the pork from the oven and discard the bone, plus any herbs and garlic, then pull meat with forks to desired consistency.

TROUT CAKES

MAKES 12 CAKES

SEAFOOD IS ONE OF MY FAVORITE THINGS TO COOK, but I rarely have the pleasure of experimenting with dishes outside of home as we practice farm-to-table cuisine at Hachland Hill. Trout and catfish are the two fresh regional fish that we showcase on our menus. After a trip to the beach with my wife's family, I returned to Nashville missing the crab cakes we had made on the trip, which is when I came up with the idea for this tasty alternative. I like to use our smoked whole trout to prepare the cakes, but your fish can be baked or grilled to achieve the same end. Serve this with our Lemon-Lovage Tartar Sauce (page 232).

4 garlic chives, chopped thin

¼ cup manganji sweet red peppers, chopped

¼ cup mayonnaise

¼ cup creole mustard

1 garlic clove, minced

2 tablespoons lemon juice

½ teaspoon lemon zest

2 tablespoons capers

½ teaspoon cajun seasoning

¼ teaspoon dill weed

½ teaspoon salt

¼ teaspoon white pepper

¼ teaspoon cayenne pepper

3 ½ cups cooked trout meat, skin and bones removed

1 cup fine breadcrumbs

2 tablespoons olive oil

In a large bowl, combine chives, red pepper, mayonnaise, mustard, garlic, lemon juice and zest, capers, seasoning, dill, and cayenne and fold together with a rubber spatula. Add the trout and breadcrumbs. Fold until evenly incorporated and trout is broken up to form a dip-like consistency. Shape mixture into 12 balls and pat into small cakes, about ½-inch thick.

Preheat oven to 170 degrees. Heat the olive oil over medium heat in a heavy skillet. Working in batches, add the trout cakes to the hot oil and cook for 4 minutes or until lightly browned and heated through, flipping once while cooking. Transfer trout cakes to a paper towel-lined platter to absorb excess oil. Keep warm in oven until ready to serve.

HONEY HOT SMOKED CHICKEN QUARTERS

SERVES 10

I WROTE MY SENIOR THESIS ON THE COMMERCIALIZATION OF HOT CHICKEN, which was fast-tracked by a KFC campaign that touted our city's staple. My research led me to menus in New York, California, London, Australia, and Asia, all of which showcased our fiery yard bird. With the utmost respect for the patriarch, Thornton Prince, I developed a smoked chicken, hot and sweet, that became one of our most cherished items at weddings, retreats, and home delivery during the pandemic. Serve it over white bread with pickles.

FOR THE BRINE:

1 gallon water

1 cup kosher salt

1 cup light brown sugar

2 tablespoons Worcestershire

1 tablespoon black pepper

1 tablespoon cayenne pepper

1 teaspoon garlic, minced

½ teaspoon ground ginger

¼ teaspoon nutmeg

½ yellow onion, sliced

3 hot peppers, halved

FOR THE RUB:

2 teaspoons kosher salt

1 teaspoon black pepper

1 teaspoon smoked paprika

1 teaspoon cayenne pepper

½ teaspoon habanero powder

2 teaspoons garlic powder

1 tablespoon light brown sugar

FOR THE BASTE:

¼ cup ketchup

¼ cup apple cider vinegar

¼ cup light brown sugar

¾ cup yellow mustard

½ cup honey

2 teaspoons apple juice

1 tablespoon Maggi seasoning

½ cup rendered duck fat

1 teaspoon sea salt

¼ teaspoon black pepper

1 teaspoon garlic powder

½ teaspoon smoked paprika

1 tablespoon cayenne pepper

1 teaspoon habanero powder

FOR THE CHICKEN:

10 chicken quarters

SPECIAL EQUIPMENT:

Smoker or open pit; hickory wood; apple wood chips

HONEY HOT SMOKED CHICKEN QUARTERS

HOW TO SMOKE MEATS

If you do not have a wood-fired smoker, you can dig a pit the size that is required for the amount of meat you have. A small hole is about 9 inches deep, say, for a grill that's about 2 feet square. For large barbecues, I like to dig a pit about 12 to 18 inches deep, 3 to 4 feet wide and as long as you wish. Alternatively, you can build from the ground up with cinderblocks. (There are plenty of instructions online on how to create your own affordable smoking pit.)

Never start to barbecue until your fire and coals have died down. Keep a fire of hickory wood (or preferred wood) going to continue feeding coals to the pit. This fire should be close to the pit. We call this the feeder fire.

We use heavy chicken wire frames to stretch across our pits. These should be a few inches above the embers. New broom or mop heads are used to brush large portions of meat with the sop. Warm salted water is used to baste the meat until it gets hot enough to keep away insects and flies.

Allow 12 to 18 hours to cook large pieces of meat over an open pit. Whole fish is quick and will take as little as 1 to 2 hours depending on the size. Chicken leg quarters will take about 5 hours.

(continued from previous page)

MAKE THE BRINE: Heat all of the brine ingredients in a large pot, stirring constantly, until the sugar has dissolved. Remove from heat and cool to room temperature.

MAKE THE RUB: Combine all ingredients together in a bowl until evenly blended. Set aside at room temperature.

MAKE THE BASTE: Combine all baste ingredients in a small pot and bring to a light boil, stirring constantly. Remove from heat and allow to cool. Refrigerate until ready to use.

MAKE THE CHICKEN: Place chicken quarters in a large pan and pour brine over top until meat is completely submerged. Cover and refrigerate for 5 hours. In a cauldron or pit, fire up hickory wood and let it burn until it turns grey in color, then break up into medium-sized chunks. Add wood, as needed, to keep the feeder fire stocked with embers for transferring to the smoker. While the hickory is burning down, soak apple wood chips in water for 1 hour.

Remove chicken from brine and lightly rinse with cool water, then pat pieces dry with a paper towel. Cover the chicken pieces with the rub, massaging the meat all over and carefully sprinkling some under the skins. Remove the wood chips from the water and pat dry with paper towels.

Place the quarters onto the smoker grate and add the prepared embers below, but not directly underneath the chicken (you want indirect heat). Evenly disperse a handful of the soaked wood chips on top of the embers and quickly close the smoker with its flu just barely open.

Replenish with fresh embers from the feeder fire and more soaked wood chips every hour until done, 5 to 6 hours. With a small mop head or brush, kiss the quarters with baste every 45 minutes, leaving them untouched for the last 30 minutes of cooking. Serve hot or at room temperature.

SUNCHOKE BRATKARTOFFELN

SERVES 10

AS MUCH FUN AS IT IS FOR ME TO FUSE TRADITIONAL SOUTHERN CUISINE—and especially Phila's country cooking—with the amazing and diverse foodways I absorbed in Asia and Africa, I also strive to pay homage to my Hach family German roots. Bratkartoffeln, or simply German fries, is one ancestral dish that I've enjoyed making with many different adaptations. This is one of my favorite variations in the winter when sunchokes are available from local farmers.

I wasn't familiar with sunchokes, also called Jerusalem artichokes, until I purchased a few pounds from one farm out of sheer curiosity. Since then, I've used them in soups, dips, and even pastries. My wife and I ate dinner one Valentine's Day at chef Dan Barber's Blue Hill at Stone Barns, and his sunchoke interpretation of a twice-baked potato blew my mind. I immediately started thinking of a sunchoke variation of hash browns, which brought me back to Bratkartoffeln.

I've left potatoes in this dish for the sake of tradition, but the chokes bring new life to it. Sausage or bacon is common in the German preparation, which prompted me to make it my own with smoked hog jowl for a slight nod to the South. This recipe is great as it stands, but topping it with a poached egg takes it to new heights for a hearty breakfast. Ladling Welsh Rarebit (page 50) over it is my guilty pleasure—but that usually induces a food coma, followed by a long run.

(continued on next page)

(continued from previous page)

1 gallon water

1 ½ teaspoons fresh lemon juice

3 pounds sunchokes*

1 pound (about 2 large) yukon gold potatoes

6 tablespoons olive oil, divided

1 pound smoked hog jowl, cut into lardons

2 red onions, diced

2 red bell peppers, diced

4 garlic cloves, minced

1 teaspoon smoked sweet paprika

2 tablespoons fresh thyme leaves

3 teaspoons grated lemon rind

1 ½ teaspoons kosher salt

½ teaspoon black pepper

*NOTE: You can also substitute Brussels sprouts.

Combine the water, lemon juice, sunchokes, and potatoes in a large pot over high heat and bring to a boil. Reduce the heat and simmer for about 30 minutes or until vegetables are tender. Strain vegetables and let cool. Peel the sunchokes, then cut chokes and potatoes into cubes.

Place a large cast-iron skillet over medium-high heat and add 2 tablespoons oil. Add the lardons and cook for about 5 minutes. Add another tablespoon of the oil, along with the onions, peppers, and garlic and cook for 5 more minutes. Spoon mixture into a bowl and set aside.

Wipe the skillet clean, then add the remaining oil, sunchokes, and potatoes and cook for about 8 minutes over medium-high heat, nudging them around occasionally. Add the jowl mixture, paprika, thyme, lemon rind, salt, and pepper to skillet and stir to incorporate. Keep warm until ready to serve.

TRINITY OF GREENS

SERVES 10

WHO DOESN'T LOVE GREENS? If someone says otherwise, it is safe to assume they've never had them proper. Some may favor turnip greens over collards, which I can understand for reasons within those folks' troubled palates. At Hachland Hill, the more, the merrier as far as our greens are concerned. Our staple greens, served at countless weddings and retreats, are comprised of turnips, collards, and mustards. If we can't get those from our farmers, we take whatever they're harvesting and fix 'em up right. Kale, dandelion, chard, Chinese broccoli, kohlrabi tops—you name it and we've braised it. I'm heavy handed on the vinegar and spice, but that's just the innate spunk of Phila coming out in me.

2 bunches turnip greens

2 bunches collard greens

2 bunches red mustard greens

1 pound hog jowl

6 quarts water

3 quarts apple cider vinegar

3 tablespoons red pepper flakes (I like Calabrian chiles)

3 tablespoons garlic powder

½ cup plus 1 tablespoon salt

¾ cup sugar

6 tablespoons soy sauce

3 tablespoons prepared horseradish

3 tablespoons honey

Wash the greens three times with water, rubbing them with kosher salt during the rinsing process, then pat dry. Strip the greens away from their stems and chop into small-to-medium-sized pieces. Place greens in a large pot with the remaining ingredients and whisk to combine. Cook over medium-low heat for 1 hour, then remove the jowl. Cut the jowl into lardons and fry over low heat in a small skillet until a nice crust forms. Continue to cook the greens for 1 ½ more hours. Strain the greens, reserving about 6 tablespoons liquid. Combine the fried jowl, greens, and reserved liquid, and simmer until ready to serve.

CANDIED SWEET POTATOES

SERVES 10

MY GRANDMOTHER, BETTY JUNE, on my mom's side of the family, was the sweet potato queen at our holiday gatherings. She was all about the brown sugar. Coincidentally her husband, my grandfather who I call Da, was the mashed potato king! I created this zippy recipe that is set apart from others with a good 'ole kick in the head from ginger and citrus.

2 cups water

2 cups sugar

8 sweet potatoes, peeled and
    thinly sliced

½ stick butter

1 teaspoon grated orange rind

Juice of ½ lemon

¼ teaspoon grated ginger

Combine water and sugar in a large pot and bring to a boil. Add the potatoes and remaining ingredients. Cook until potatoes are well cooked and candied.

ASPARAGUS TOAST *with* WHITE SAUCE

SERVES 4

THIS IS ANOTHER RECIPE THAT I CREDIT TO MY MOM'S PARENTS. Da had a little garden behind their home in Hopkinsville, Kentucky, that produced tomatoes, wheat, and asparagus. Whenever I'd visit them, Da and I would walk back through the yard to his patch of fresh produce, which was so fun for a young me with my penchant for anything outdoors as long as I ended up dirty. We'd pick bunches of asparagus and bring it back to the house to enjoy over fresh toast topped with a white gravy, which my grandparents called sauce. It's a memory that is especially dear to me now as I practice farm-to-table cuisine at Hachland Hill. It all started in "Hoptown."

1 bunch asparagus

1 scallion, diced

2 tablespoons olive oil

¼ teaspoon garlic powder

1 pinch celery salt

2 teaspoons truffle oil

¼ cup melted butter, plus ¼ stick butter

4 slices white bread

1 teaspoon salt

½ teaspoon black pepper

4 tablespoons all-purpose flour

½ cup whole milk

Preheat oven to 350 degrees. Toss the asparagus and scallion in the olive oil and place on a baking sheet. Roast for about 12 minutes until tender and just starting to crisp. Remove from oven and keep warm until ready to serve.

Whisk the garlic powder, celery salt, and truffle oil into the ¼ cup melted butter and use it to brush both sides of the bread slices. Toast bread in the oven until slightly browned, flipping once.

Place ¼ stick of butter in a saucepan over low heat, then add salt, black pepper, and flour. Whisk until smooth, then slowly add the milk, thinning to desired consistency. To serve, place the asparagus on top of the toasted bread and pour the sauce over top.

POTATO-PARSLEY ROOT MASH

SERVES 10

THIS WAS ONE OF TWO FUN SIDE DISHES that we offered to our cooking classes during the pandemic. Everyone knows mashed potatoes, but the parsley root is something new for a lot of our guests. Where there's a quart of cream, there's going to be a plate worth licking clean.

2 pounds parsley root, peeled

5 pounds yukon gold potatoes, peeled

1 quart heavy cream

½ teaspoon garlic powder

1 teaspoon black pepper

1 tablespoon salt

1 stick butter, room temperature

Cut parsley root and potatoes into 2-inch pieces. Place in a pot and cover with cream. Add garlic powder, black pepper, and salt. Stir with a rubber spatula to evenly distribute the seasonings. Bring to a boil over medium heat, stirring occasionally until the roots and potatoes are tender enough to break with the spatula. Strain the vegetables from the cream and add to a stand mixer fitted with a whisk attachment. Mix on low speed and add the butter. Increase the speed to medium and continue to whip until smooth. Serve warm.

Potato-Parsley Root Mash pictured on page 114.

PEPPER JELLY-GLAZED CARROTS

SERVES 6

THIS IS ANOTHER HIT from our Covid-era cooking classes. Learning to cook carrots is okay and all. But making your own pepper jelly and returning home with a jar to glaze your carrots in—and for your Triscuits and cream cheese? That's the ticket! These carrots are a wonderful accompaniment to lamb or venison.

1 cup dried red Slovakia paprika peppers*

6 dried habanada peppers*

2 cups apple cider vinegar

7 cups sugar

2 envelopes fruit pectin (I use Certo)

2 pounds baby carrots

1 (10 ½ ounce) can chicken broth

2 tablespoons butter

***NOTE**: You can substitute other hot peppers as desired

Remove stems and about half of the seeds from the peppers and place in a food processor along with the vinegar. Puree, leaving some bits whole for color contrast. Add the vinegar-pepper mixture to a pot along with the sugar and bring to a roaring boil over medium heat, stirring occasionally. Boil for 4 minutes. Stir in the fruit pectin. Bring back to a boil for 1 minute longer. Ladle jelly into warmed jars, wipe the rims clean and seal with lids. Process the filled jars in hot water for 5 minutes. (This should yield about 7 half-pint jars.)

In a skillet over medium heat, combine carrots and chicken broth and bring to a boil. Lower to a simmer, stirring often. Once carrots are crisp and tender and broth has reduced to about a ¼ cup, stir in butter and 1 jar of pepper jelly. Continue cooking the carrots while moving constantly with a rubber spatula for 5 more minutes until mixture is thickened and carrots are glazed.

Pepper Jelly-Glazed Carrots pictured on page 124.

PIMENTO CHEESE SQUASH AU GRATIN

SERVES 15 TO 20

ASIDE FROM COOKING CLASSES, Hachland Hill launched family-sized meals for home delivery at the start of the pandemic. This was a really popular offering, and it has since been served to many guests at our inn. We'd cook everything up in large batches and out the door the containers would go. Children might normally shy away from a pan of squash, but they come around when there's pimento cheese and Funyons in the mix.

4 sticks unsalted butter	2 cups pimento cheese (page 59)
1 tablespoon minced garlic	1 ½ cups cream cheese
10 pounds yellow squash, thinly sliced	Finely ground Funyons and crackers
1 large yellow onion, diced	Extra sharp cheddar cheese, grated
1 tablespoon Lowry's seasoning	Sharp cheddar cheese, grated
1 teaspoon black pepper	
1 teaspoon white pepper	

Preheat oven to 350 degrees. Melt butter in a saucepan over low heat, then add the garlic. Add the squash and onion and sauté until softened. Add the Lowry's, and black and white pepper, and stir to incorporate. Pour the sautéed squash into a large bowl and let it cool slightly.

Use a spatula to fold pimento cheese and cream cheese into squash mixture until evenly incorporated and smooth. (You may also work it together with gloved hands to break up the cream cheese.) Pour into a greased casserole dish or pie pan.

Bake for about 25 minutes until bubbly with a slightly browned crust. Remove from oven and dust with the Funyon/cracker meal and sprinkle with the grated cheeses. Bake for 7 more minutes.

PHILA'S FAVORITE EGGPLANT CASSEROLE

SERVES 5

MY DAD ALWAYS RAVED ABOUT PHILA'S EGGPLANT, which he ate growing up with her. She was certainly a fan herself, too, as she deemed it her "favorite" in five of her cookbooks. This is as simple as it gets for a quick tailgate or lake weekend get together, and it is simply delicious.

1 large eggplant, peeled, cubed and boiled until tender, and drained

2 whole eggs

1 ½ cups cream

1 tablespoon onion juice

Salt and pepper, to taste

Cracker crumbs and butter for topping

Preheat oven to 350 degrees. In a bowl, combine eggplant with the remaining ingredients, except for cracker crumbs and butter. Place in casserole dish and top with cracker crumbs and dot all over with butter. Bake until firm, about 25 to 30 minutes. To brown the topping a bit, turn on the broiler for the last 2 to 3 minutes of cooking time.

TWICE-BAKED POTATOES

SERVES 12

WHENEVER PHILA MADE HER BEEF TENDERLOIN, it was almost guaranteed that a twice-baked potato would be sitting on the plate next to it. She made it a number of different ways over the years, sometimes just stuffing the potatoes and serving them cold without the second bake. I followed in her tracks and got the twice-baked potato bug when I was at Ole Miss. I reckon I made fifteen or so different varieties at the house I lived in during my sophomore year. I recall a spicy buffalo-blue cheese-sausage stuffed creation that may have been the winning spud. I laugh today at those culinary experiments, because the flavors certainly fit the profile for a crew of ravenous college guys. No matter the filling and process, it's hard to go wrong with a twice-baked potato.

6 baking potatoes, baked, halved, and scooped out of skins; skins reserved

1 stick butter

1 cup sour cream

2 tablespoons whole milk

2 tablespoons cream cheese

1 cup grated smoked gouda

1 pinch celery salt

½ teaspoon fresh dill, finely chopped

¼ teaspoon red pepper flakes

½ teaspoon Knorr granulated chicken bouillon

1 tablespoon roasted garlic, minced

1 teaspoon chives, finely chopped

Preheat oven to 350 degrees. While the potatoes are hot, whip them in a stand mixer with the butter, sour cream, milk, cheeses, and seasonings. Add more sour cream if necessary. Pipe or spoon into the hollow skins and bake for 30 minutes, or until heated through and slightly golden on top. (You can add bacon and cheese to the mix if desired.)

RUTABAGAS OVER KABOCHA

MAKES 8 SERVINGS

I MADE THIS DISH FOR A FAMILY THANKSGIVING not long after taking the reins at Hachland Hill. It was when I first started to get "chef-y," and it was a favorite dish that year. I developed the recipe more over the years until I was satisfied with what is now a popular dish for our guests on the Hill.

3 kabocha squash

2 teaspoons salt

1 teaspoon white pepper

2 small garlic cloves, minced

½ white mango turmeric root, peeled and grated

1 ½ cups heavy cream

3 tablespoons melted butter

1 cup rendered beef fat

3 rutabagas, peeled and cubed

1 shallot, diced

Balsamic reduction

Chili oil

Basil microgreens

Preheat oven to 400 degrees. Cut the tops from the squash, slice in half, and remove the seeds and pulp. Rub the insides of the squash with salt and pepper. Fill the bottom of a baking dish with a ½ inch of boiling water and place squash cut-side down in the water. Bake for about 30 minutes or until tender. Remove and let cool.

Scrape meat from cooked squash into a food processor. Add the garlic and turmeric and pulse to combine. While machine is running, pour the cream and butter through the top of the processor and blend until smooth.

Heat the beef fat in a heavy skillet over medium heat. Add the rutabagas and shallot and fry until tender. Season with salt and pepper. Strain the rutabagas and shallot. To serve, top the warm squash puree with the rutabaga mixture. Garnish with balsamic reduction, chili oil, and basil microgreens.

MAGIC MUSHROOMS

SERVES 6

I WAS NEVER HUGE ON MUSHROOMS GROWING UP. It wasn't that I disliked them, but it was never something that Phila or my mom made for us children. Once I was cooking for Hachland Hill and learning about all of the amazing varieties available from a local farmer and friend, David Wells of Henosis, I started to create a new mushroom dish just about every week. A pioppino mushroom German potato salad was one of the first creations. Our bed-and-breakfast guests are often treated to smoked sausage and king oyster mushroom gravy over poached eggs on toast. The possibilities are endless with "ground scallops." They're the perfect complement to just about any plate.

1 large scallion, halved and sliced very thin

4 garlic cloves, minced

1 ½ sticks unsalted butter, melted

½ teaspoon salt

½ teaspoon black pepper

¼ teaspoon mustard powder

¼ teaspoon dried thyme

½ teaspoon smoked paprika

2 teaspoons Pommery barrel-aged red wine vinegar

1 cup black garlic shoyu

6 cups mixed mushrooms, chopped (I like king oysters, maitake, lion's mane, and shiitake)

½ teaspoon lemon zest

1 teaspoon fresh dill, chopped fine

Grated Parmesan (optional)

In a large skillet, simmer the scallion and garlic in the butter for about 10 minutes. Add the seasonings, vinegar, and black garlic shoyu, stirring to combine. Fold in the mushrooms until evenly coated and cook over low heat for about 1 ½ hours, stirring every 10 minutes, until volume has reduced by ⅔. Add the lemon zest and dill just before serving. Top with grated parmesan if desired.

SPICY ROASTED OKRA
with LEMON-THYME AÏOLI

SERVES 6

MY FAVORITE SNACK IS PICKLED OKRA. I've been known to place a mason jar full of them in the drink console of my truck during long road trips! I wanted to create something special to introduce the wonders of okra to all of those who skip over them at the store. This side is sure to please, and it makes for a great appetizer, too.

1-1 ½ pounds okra, preferably a longer variety

1 teaspoon cumin seeds

1 teaspoon coriander seeds

½ teaspoon madras curry powder

½ teaspoon sweet Hungarian paprika

¼ teaspoon black pepper

1 teaspoon sea salt

1 tablespoon yellow cornmeal

1 tablespoon lime juice

2 tablespoons extra-virgin olive oil

Lemon-thyme aïoli (page 230)

Cornbread croutons (refer to Hachland Caesar, page 86)

Cilantro microgreens, to garnish

Preheat oven to 350 degrees. Wash okra and dry very well with a paper towel. Slice the okra in half lengthwise. Evenly disperse them on a roasting rack set upon a sheet tray.

In a skillet, toast the coriander and cumin for about 5 minutes or until deeply aromatic. Using a coffee grinder, pulse the toasted seeds into a coarse powder. In a small bowl, combine ground seeds with the remaining spices and mix well.

Sprinkle the spice mixture, cornmeal, lime juice, and olive oil over the okra, and massage it all together for a good even coat. Bake for 20 minutes, stirring the okra about halfway through. The okra should turn a dark green and hold the spices well when done. To serve, drizzle with lemon-thyme aïoli, then sprinkle with crumbled cornbread crouton and top with microgreens.

Chapter 4

BREADS & SUCH

Phila's Story
PART 4

PHILA PUBLISHED 18 COOKBOOKS over the course of her career. The book she originally authored in 1974, *Kountry Kooking*, went on to become Opryland Hotel's official cookbook for years. She considered herself an authority on the craft of country cooking. She told me, when we cooked together, that the methods were unique to Tennessee and contrary to a generic Southern style or that of the coasts. "Using what you have, country cooking," she said. "Though I've written near 20 cookbooks, I never have to open one because country cooking is the mind's recipe." The book, reprinted in 1983 as *Kountry Kooking: For City Folk (Official Cookbook of Opryland U.S.A.)*, was followed by another in the same year that was named *Plantation Recipes and Kountry Kooking (Official Cookbook of Opryland U.S.A.).*

Through these book partnerships with Opryland, she met her long-time friend, Rudy Caduff, in 1982. Rudy, a Swedish entrepreneur who was like-minded in his business endeavors, served as the director of catering at Opryland from 1978 to 1999 and ran a restaurant in Nashville, Nick and Rudy's Steakhouse, from 2000 to 2008.

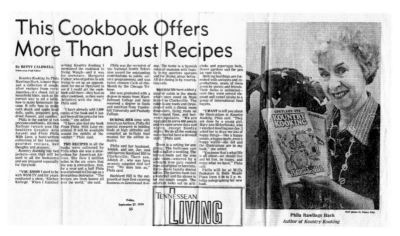

Many articles covered Phila and her cookbooks.

Lamar Alexander (left) with Phila and Alex Haley (right)

Rudy, who I joke with about being the busiest retired person I know, lends a helping hand to me at Hachland Hill when we have larger catering orders. We often chat on our way to a job about that sort of work ethic, characteristic of his and Phila's generation, that seems lost today. I strive to always be humble and open to learning, putting in the blood, sweat, and tears as a testament to the work ethic that she instilled in my father that was passed on to me.

Rudy refers to his and Phila's shared stories as "catering war stories." One such story, set in 1986 at Alex Haley's home involved some fast think-ing on Phila's part. Haley, a historical writer, is best known for authoring *The Malcom X Autobiography* in 1965 and *Roots: The Saga of an American Family* in 1976, which was later adapted by ABC as a TV mini-series. Lamar Alexander, Governor of Tennessee at the time, was one of many esteemed guests at Haley's home that evening. He went on to serve as the fifth U.S. secretary of education before becoming a U.S. senator, a chairman of the Senate Republican Conference, and chairman of the Senate Committee on Health, Education, Labor, and Pensions. His happiness with the meal was a testament to Phila practicing what she preached about country cooking.

Alexander was overseeing the "Tennessee Homecoming," a tourism event in which local communities launched numerous projects that focused on state and local heritage. Haley and country music royalty Minnie Pearl were co-chairs for the party, put on in support of Alexander's campaign.

Ruth Williams' brother, John Fletcher

They hosted 300 guests at Haley's home in East Tennessee, and called for Phila to cater the event. (This particular celebration was the namesake of her *Homecoming Cookbook: Famous Parties, People, Places* published in 1986.)

While driving to Haley's home for the event, one hour from their destination, Ruth recalls that one of her fellow employees realized that no one had loaded the pies. When they sheepishly admitted their mistake, Phila went ballistic—but then she did what she was good at doing and pulled it off impromptu. After whirling into a Kroger parking lot, Phila frantically and confidentially marched inside with her staff at her sides. "Miss Phila announced to some checkout person that she had done the grand opening for this store and that she was going to use their kitchen for a minute. Asking no one's permission, she took over the kitchen and within 45 minutes had made the required fudge, chess, and pecan pies to accommodate her 300 guests," Rudy told me. I can tell you that my grandmother never did the grand opening for any Krogers, but she did commandeer that one!

Quick on her feet and using what she had at her disposal, she exemplified her country cooking ideals in that moment. Once the pies had been served, Phila recalled Alexander commenting on the deliciousness and warmth of his piece of fudge pie.

"I revealed our secret to him alone, and he said, 'I'll never tell.' The evening was a success," she said.

As worthy of Rudy's "catering war stories" as any, another of Phila's tales involved yet another Tennessee governor, as well as an aerial stunt and Ruth's brother, John Fletcher.

Former Governor Ray Blanton, who held office from 1975 to 1979 (he was succeeded by Alexander), was successful at recruiting foreign international companies to Tennessee. He also created the Department of Tourism, the first in the nation.

Blanton was hosting a Sudanese trade representative for a weeklong tour of Tennessee 's historic sites and homes. As a way to teach about each respective stop, he invited the local mayors and dignitaries to join them for meals. Brooks Parker, Blanton's administrative aide and press secretary, and one of Phila's longest friends, saw to it that she cater the whole week of meals during their travels. Parker told me in an interview that there were people from Africa, the Middle East, anywhere and everywhere, and Phila had types of menus that were American but that also reflected the cuisines of the countries with representation present at each meal.

On the day the tour began, she was headed to a historic mansion in Columbia, Tennessee, where the meal would be served that day. Phila, running through the menu with me like she had cooked it yesterday, said she prepared a Southern and Sudanese fused feast, embodied by her classic fried chicken modified with African essentials like peanut oil, garlic, and hot pepper to batter the breasts. It was complemented by her Tennessee take on "moukhbaza," a dish made from banana paste that is often decorated with a fresh pepper sauce.

She drove some of her staff members in her station wagon, while John Fletcher drove the catering van, which was filled with all of the food. John missed their exit, prompting Phila to inform Blanton and Parker that her driver and all of the food was missing. She remembers Governor Blanton looking at her and giving her assurance that they would find him. In no time, he dispatched a Tennessee Highway Patrol helicopter to search for John. Aimlessly driving down the interstate, John spotted a low flying helicopter that was drawing nearer in his rearview mirror. The helicopter did a flyby, before circling back around behind the van. "On its second pass, John told me, the helicopter dipped down in front of the van, tilting here and there to signal him," Ruth shared her brother's account with me. "Right then, he knew it was Miss Phila."

Following his escort in the sky, John arrived in Columbia, and the dinner proved to be a tremendous success.

HH BISCUITS

MAKES 14 BISCUITS

BISCUITS ARE AS MUCH A PART OF HACHLAND HILL as the woods and the 150-year-old tobacco barn. It was the one recipe that I didn't need a French chef to teach me at school, because I had been schooled in this Southern staple by the one and only Ruth Williams. She wasn't hanging up her apron until I could make biscuits with my eyes closed and a hand behind my back. Also, let it be known, Southern biscuits are *round*. I've grown tired of all the square biscuit nonsense. The pioneering bakers, from simpler times past in the South, used cans to cut their round biscuits.

4 ¼ cups all-purpose flour

2 tablespoons baking powder

1 teaspoon salt

1 ½ sticks unsalted butter

¾ cup whole milk

¼ cup heavy cream

¼ cup buttermilk

Heavy cream for brushing

Melted butter for brushing

Preheat oven to 350 degrees. Combine the flour, baking powder, and salt in a bowl. Cut the butter with a bench scraper or knife into dice-sized cubes. Cut the cubed butter into the dry ingredients until it gets down to pea-size pieces. Add the liquid ingredients, just to combine; do not overmix. Roll out the dough to about ¾-inch thick on a lightly floured work surface. Cut into desired shapes. Place on a sheet tray lined with parchment paper. Brush with heavy cream. Bake until lightly colored on top, about 12 to 15 minutes. Remove from oven and brush generously with melted butter while they are still warm.

HH SCONES

MAKES 8 LARGE SCONES (OR 16 SMALL)

I LEARNED LONDON'S HOTEL SAVOY SIGNATURE SCONE RECIPE during my bread and pastry courses in New York. Its base recipe is one that I keep close to my chest. I have worked that recipe a million times now, with savory applications, sweet remedies, and even corn-bread versions as a nod to the South. Scones are in abundance for our bed-and-breakfast guests, and not one batch is ever the same. I make our scones on the fly, improvising with whatever is available, to create a unique treat every time in the spirit of Phila's "country cooking" philosophy.

2 ½ cups bread flour

1 ½ tablespoons baking powder

¼ cup sugar

¼ teaspoon salt

1 stick unsalted butter

½-¾ cup white chocolate
(or other desired filling
such as fruit, herbs, cheese,
sausage, or other)

Zest of 1 lemon

2 teaspoons dried rosemary

1 whole egg

1 egg yolk

1 teaspoon pure vanilla extract
(if desired)

½-¾ cup heavy cream, plus more
for brushing

Sugar for sprinkling (or use
desired seasoning)

(continued on next page)

(continued from previous page)

Preheat oven to 350 degrees. Mix the flour, baking powder, sugar, and salt together in a large bowl. Cut the butter with a bench scraper or knife into dice-sized cubes. Cut the cubed butter into to the dry ingredients until it gets down to pea-sized pieces. (If it is cut up too fine, the final product will not be as flaky.)

Add the white chocolate, lemon zest, and rosemary (or your choice of filling) to the flour mixture. Lightly whisk the whole egg, egg yolk, vanilla, and ½ to ¾ cup cream together in a small bowl to combine. Add the liquid ingredients to the dry ingredients all at once. Mix with your hands until a dough forms. (Do not overwork, it should be soft and just come together.)

Turn the dough out onto a lightly floured work surface. Pat and round out the dough with your hands until it's ¾-inch thick. (These raw scones may be refrigerated for two days or frozen for one month.)

Using a bench scraper, cut the dough round in half then cut each half into quarters, like pie slices. Place the scones on a sheet tray lined with parchment paper, then brush with heavy cream and sprinkle with sugar (or desired seasoning). Bake the scones for 10 to 15 minutes, until golden brown on the bottoms and around the edges. Remove from the oven and brush with more cream while still hot, and sprinkle with more sugar.

HH CONTINENTAL MUFFINS

MAKES 12 MUFFINS

WE LOVE OUR MUFFINS ON THE HILL. They are a standard item on our continental break-fast. We usually provide them in our guests' in-room snack boxes, too. I often joke that the muffin man actually lives on Rawlings Road. You can also save a step by scrapping the tur-meric and apples altogether. Simply fold some fresh blueberries into the batter with a rubber spatula before scooping it into your tins, and you'll have an instant classic.

FOR THE STREUSEL:

¼ cup melted unsalted butter

¼ teaspoon pure vanilla extract

¾ cup all-purpose flour

4 ½ tablespoons sugar

1 tablespoon cinnamon

FOR THE APPLES:

½ turmeric root, peeled

1 tablespoon sugar

1 teaspoon pure vanilla extract

½ stick unsalted butter

3 apples, peeled and cut into small cubes

FOR THE MUFFINS:

2 ¼ sticks unsalted butter

½ cup sugar

2 whole eggs

¼ teaspoon hazelnut extract or syrup

2 ¼ cups all-purpose flour

¾ tablespoon baking powder

1 teaspoon salt

¾ cup buttermilk

Dried currants

(continued on next page)

(continued from previous page)

MAKE THE STREUSEL: In a bowl, combine the melted butter with the remaining ingredients. Chill until the crumble is cold.

MAKE THE APPLES: In a food processor, pulse the turmeric, sugar, and vanilla until a paste forms. Melt the butter in a skillet over low heat. Add the apples and increase to medium heat, then sauté until tender. Add the turmeric mixture and simmer for 5 minutes more. Strain the apples and set them aside on a paper towel-lined tray, allowing them to come to room temperature.

MAKE THE MUFFINS: Preheat oven to 350 degrees. Coat a muffin pan with non-stick baking spray. In a mixer fitted with a paddle attachment, cream together the butter and sugar until light and fluffy. Add the eggs and extract one at a time, mixing after each addition. Alternate adding the dry ingredients and the buttermilk. Mix until just combined. Fold the desired amount of the currants and turmeric-apples into the batter with a rubber spatula.

Using an ice cream scoop, drop batter into the prepared pan. Break up the chilled crumble topping to avoid any large clumps, then sprinkle over the muffins. Lightly press it down into the muffin batter, without creating a crater, and sprinkle again with any leftover crumbs. Bake for about 25 minutes. Remove from oven and let cool for 10 or so minutes to take on their shape and keep from falling apart, then tap the pan onto the counter and invert so that they come out of their tins.

BRIOCHE DOUGH

MAKES ENOUGH FOR 3 LOAVES, 20 BUNS, 50 ROLLS, OR 16 SWEET ROLLS

BRIOCHE IS MY FAVORITE DOUGH, probably because it is chock-full of butter! It is so versatile and simple enough for anyone to do at home without qualms. Our retreats can always count on sliced brioche loaf bread being present when there is a soup, salad, and sandwich buffet. We also use it for our cinnamon rolls, dinner rolls, and so many other baked items. The smell of fresh bread in the oven is as warm a welcome as it gets for a guest walking into the inn.

3 ¾ heaping cups bread flour (almost 4 cups)

½ cup water

¼ cup heavy cream

2 whole eggs

2 teaspoons dry yeast

4 ¾ tablespoons sugar

½ tablespoon salt

1 ½ sticks chilled unsalted butter (cut into small cubes)

Note: To check the development of the gluten, gently tug the dough with your thumb and pointer finger. You're good to go if it opens up a hole that you can see through with the perimeter intact. This is called "pulling a window" in the baking world.

Combine the flour, water, cream, eggs, and yeast in the bowl of a stand mixer fitted with a paddle attachment. Mix on low speed for 2 minutes. Add the sugar and salt and mix for 1 minute more. Replace the paddle attachment with a hook attachment. Mix on medium speed for 5 to 6 minutes to fully develop the gluten in the dough. Check the gluten development by "pulling a window" in the dough (see note).

Replace the hook attachment with a paddle attachment. With the mixer running on low speed, gradually add the cubed butter and mix until incorporated. Work the dough until it is smooth and satiny. It will be necessary to scrape the dough off the paddle and the sides of the bowl several times during the mixing. The final dough should completely come away from the sides of the bowl and have a smooth texture and developed elasticity.

Place the dough in a lightly oiled bowl, cover with plastic wrap, and let rest to ferment for 1 hour. Punch down the dough and turn it out onto a parchment paper-lined half-sheet pan. Flatten the dough and wrap the pan with plastic wrap. Refrigerate overnight.

PUMPKIN POUND CAKE

SERVES 14

MY BROTHER TELLS ME that this is one his favorite things that I make. While it is hard to beat fresh baked confections, he argues that this one is even better after it has been chilled for a day. I have to agree with him. The little extra crunch from a day of resting in the refrigerator makes this pound cake delightful.

FOR THE PUMPKIN CRÈME PÂTISSIÈRE:

1 pumpkin

1 quart whole milk

1 vanilla bean, split and scraped

1 ¼ cups sugar, divided

2 whole eggs

4 egg yolks

¾-1 cup pastry powder (you can substitute cornstarch)

FOR THE POUND CAKE:

4 sticks unsalted butter

2 ¼ cups sugar

2 teaspoons coffee extract

7 whole eggs

3 ⅔ cups all-purpose flour

1 tablespoon baking powder

1 cup chopped walnuts

MAKE THE PÂTISSIÈRE: Preheat oven to 400 degrees Cut off the top of the pumpkin and remove the seeds and pulp. Fill the bottom of a baking dish with boiling water and set the pumpkin inside, cut-side down. Bake the pumpkin for about 45 minutes or until tender. Scoop out the pumpkin's cooked meat, place in a food processor, and puree until smooth. Reserve in a bowl at room temperature.

Lay a sheet or two of plastic wrap inside a half sheet pan to completely cover its surface. In a medium saucepan over medium heat, combine the milk, scraped vanilla bean, and half of the sugar. Bring the mixture to a boil, stirring occasionally with a rubber spatula.

While that mixture heats, in another bowl combine the whole eggs and egg yolks with the remaining sugar and pastry cream powder. Whisk hard until the mixture is smooth with no lumps and turns pale yellow. Whisking constantly, pour ⅓ of the boiling milk into the egg mixture to temper it. Add the tempered egg mixture to the saucepan, along with the remaining milk and turn heat to medium-high. Quickly fold in the pumpkin puree and boil for 2 minutes, stirring constantly to avoid burning the bottom, until it is fully cooked and has thickened to your desired consistency. Remove the crème pâtissière from the heat and transfer it to the plastic wrap-covered sheet pan. Remove the vanilla bean and discard. Gently smooth out the mixture with a rubber spatula, then pull the edges of the plastic wrap together tightly overlapping to prevent a skin from forming on top of the pastry cream. Invert the wrapped product and set aside to cool completely.

MAKE THE POUND CAKE: Preheat oven to 325 degrees. In a stand mixer fitted with a paddle attachment, cream together the butter and sugar until light and fluffy. Add the extract followed by the eggs one at a time with the mixer running, increasing the speed between each addition to fully incorporate. Add the flour and baking powder a little at a time and blend until it all comes together (it may be necessary to scrape the sides and bottom of the bowl a few times). Fold in the walnuts with a rubber spatula.

Coat one bundt cake pan with nonstick baking spray, then spoon the batter into it, filling it about halfway. Smooth out the surface with an offset spatula. Line a pitcher with a gallon Ziploc bag and fill it with the cooled pumpkin crème pâtissière. Cut off one corner of the bag with scissors, about 1-inch deep. Pipe the pastry cream into the center of the cake batter, going all the way around the pan. Using the remaining batter, fill in the space between the cream and inner and outer sides of the pan, then gently top it so that the pâtissière filling is no longer visible. Lightly smooth out the surface with an offset spatula.

Bake for 15 minutes, then reduce the temperature to 300 degrees and continue baking until done and a skewer comes out clean. Remove from the oven and let it cool. Invert the cake pan onto your work surface and glaze with icing if desired. Slice and enjoy.

Pumpkin Pound Cake pictured on page 166.

FOOLPROOF PIE CRUST

MAKES 4 TO 6 PIE SHELLS

THIS IS MY GREAT GRANDMOTHER'S RECIPE, and I haven't changed even a pinch. There is a reason people cherish ancient recipe cards handed down from generation to generation in their families—they work.

4 cups cake flour

2 teaspoons salt

1 tablespoon sugar

1 ¾ cups lard or shortening

1 egg

½ cup plus 1 tablespoon ice cold water

Sift together dry ingredients. Cut in shortening and mix together with a fork until it is as fine as meal. Add egg and water, mixing until it is all evenly incorporated. Shape into 4 to 6 balls, depending on the size of your pie pan. Chill in refrigerator for 15 minutes or more. Grease pie pan with non-stick spray or oil. Roll out the dough onto floured wax paper and line pie pan with pastry, gently pressing down to fit it in and creasing the edges along the pan's rim. Carefully cut the runoff pastry away with a paring knife. Crimp the edges of the dough with your fingers or a fork to achieve your desired look.

CROISSANT DOUGH

MAKES ENOUGH DOUGH FOR 18 CROISSANTS

THIS IS A TRICKY DOUGH TO PERFECT, but you can show off to all of your friends at your dinner parties once you get it nailed down. Phila used to always serve the most buttery croissants sitting in a pool of au jus next to her beef entrees. It is a taste and texture that is hard to beat. Practice makes perfect.

2 tablespoons (30 grams) unsalted butter, plus 1 ½ cups (345 grams) for dough

6 cups (750 grams) bread flour

½ cup (100 grams) sugar

2 ½ tablespoons (38 grams) fresh yeast

1 ¼ cups (285 grams) water

⅔ cup (150 grams) milk

2 ¾ teaspoons (15 grams) salt

MAKE BEURRE EN POMADE: Heat butter in a microwave safe bowl just enough so that it can be whisked with a fork to mayonnaise consistency.

PREPARE A DÉTREMPE: Combine the flour, sugar, beurre en pommade, and yeast in a stand mixer fitted with the paddle attachment. Combine the water and milk in a separate bowl and stir to combine. Add the liquid ingredients to the dry ingredients and mix on low speed just to combine. Fit the mixer with the dough hook attachment and add the salt, then increase speed to medium and mix for about 5 minutes until a smooth, sticky dough comes together. Round the dough on your counter and cover it with plastic wrap, then let it rise for 1 hour.

(continued on next page)

CROISSANT DOUGH

(continued from previous page)

Flatten the dough and shape it into a 12-inch square. Wrap it in plastic wrap and refrigerate for about 25 minutes. Temper the remaining butter in parchment paper, beating on it with a rolling pin and then smoothing it out into a 6- by 12-inch beurrage (or block of butter). Place the beurrage at the center of your dough square, carefully pulling the parchment paper away from the butter, then start on the pâton, which is butter bound by dough at the seam like a book. Bring the dough together to wrap it around the beurrage and completely cover the butter without overlapping at the seam. Lightly beat on the dough with a rolling pin to make the butter more extendable and close off the seam (don't be afraid to show the dough who is boss, just make sure the butter doesn't come through anywhere).

Roll the pâton into a 30- by 8-inch rectangle and perform a double turn by folding the rolled-out dough like a blanket to overlap several times. Rotate the dough so the spine (like a thick book) is on your left and roll it out again into a 30- by 8-inch rectangle. Perform a single turn. Rotate it again and roll into a tight 12- by 8-inch rectangle. Wrap the dough with plastic wrap and refrigerate for at least 3 hours, or overnight.

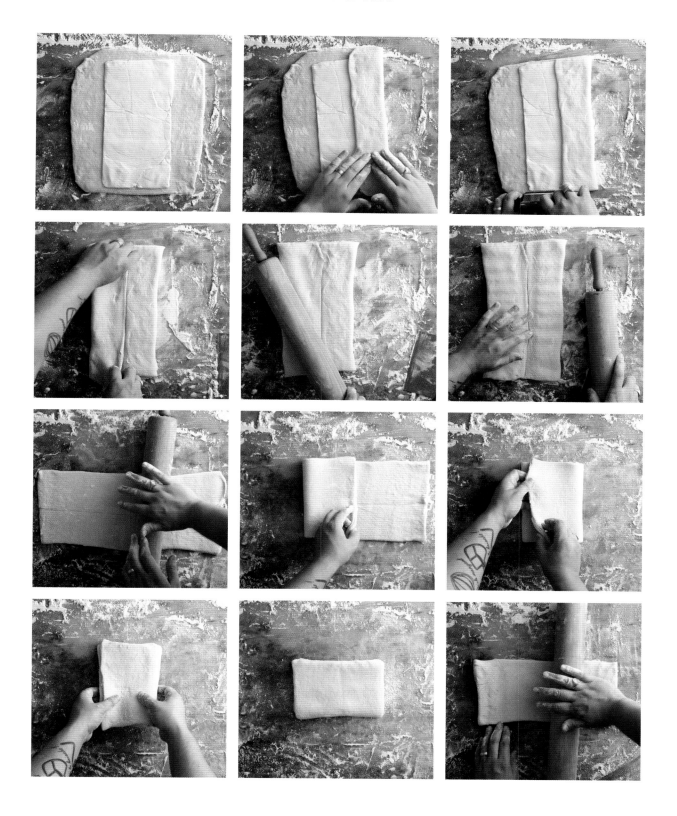

TENNESSEE WHISKEY-ORANGE SWEET ROLLS

MAKES 8 ROLLS

PILLSBURY ORANGE SWEET ROLLS WERE MY FAVORITE BREAKFAST as a child. I really just liked to lick the icing off the spoon. Nostalgia took its toll and I created my own adult version that can be served at breakfast or warm with a scoop of ice cream for dessert.

FOR THE CHEESE FILLING:

1⅔ cups cream cheese

4 tablespoons sugar

1 egg yolk

4 tablespoons pastry cream powder (or use cornstarch)

Zest of 1 orange

1 teaspoon vanilla extract

FOR THE TOPPING:

⅔ cup dark brown sugar

⅓ cup unsalted butter

2 tablespoons plus 1 teaspoon honey

¼ cup whiskey

½ cup pecans, chopped

¼ teaspoon nutmeg, ground

FOR THE STICKY BUNS:

1 teaspoon cinnamon

¼ teaspoon ground cloves

¼ teaspoon ground allspice

¼ teaspoon ground nutmeg

⅓ cup light brown sugar

Brioche dough (page 174)

2 tablespoons melted butter

FOR THE ICING:

1 vanilla bean

1 ½ cups powdered sugar, sifted

1 tablespoon buttermilk

3 tablespoons orange juice or water

2 teaspoons orange zest

(continued on next page)

TENNESSEE WHISKEY-ORANGE SWEET ROLLS

(continued from previous page)

MAKE THE CHEESE FILLING: Blend the cream cheese and sugar together in a stand mixer fitted with a paddle attachment. Add the egg yolk and continue to blend until just combined, scraping the sides and bottom of the bowl several times to ensure it is evenly mixed. Add the pastry cream powder, orange zest, and vanilla, then mix to evenly incorporate (scraping the sides again between mixing for a smooth product). Allow the filling to warm to room temperature.

MAKE THE TOPPING: Place all of the ingredients in a saucepan and cook over low heat, stirring until the sugar has melted and it is evenly combined. Remove from stove and allow it to cool slightly. Pour the mixture into a bundt cake pan coated in non-stick baking spray, then set it aside.

MAKE THE STICKY BUNS: Preheat the oven to 375 degrees. Combine all of the spices and sugar in a small bowl. Roll brioche dough into a thin rectangle, about 12 by 16 inches. Brush the dough sheet with the melted butter and sprinkle with the spice mixture. Line a pitcher with a gallon Ziploc bag and fill it with the cheese filling. Cut off one corner of the bag with scissors, about 1-inch deep. Pipe the filling in a straight line parallel to the long side of the rectangle, from end to end, leaving just enough space from the edge so that the dough can be tightly tented over the filling. Gently roll the dough from the long side up toward the top to create a log. Cut the log into 8 equal pieces with a bench scraper and place them cut-side down in the prepared cake pan.

Proof the buns for 20 minutes at 75 to 80 degrees. Place the pan the oven and bake for 20 to 25 minutes. (If the tops start to brown too much, tent with foil and continue to bake.)

Remove from the oven and let the rolls rest in their pan for 5 minutes. Place a roasting rack on top of a parchment paper-lined sheet tray, then invert the cake pan onto the rack (it is important to do this step while the caramel topping is still warm).

MAKE THE ICING: Slice the vanilla bean in half and scrape out the inside with a paring knife. Combine the sugar, buttermilk, orange juice, and zest in a bowl and whisk until there are no lumps. Add vanilla as desired (¼ teaspoon is more than enough). Whisk all together to evenly incorporate for a smooth and shiny final product. Ladle over the cooled sticky buns and let cool until the icing firms up.

HOMINY-JALAPEÑO SPOON BREAD

SERVES 8

IT IS HARD TO DESCRIBE SPOON BREAD. Contrary to its name, it is more similar in consistency to a savory pudding, such as Yorkshire, than bread. The addition of hominy and jalapeño gives this a unique distinction from traditional versions. Serve it alongside a hearty pot roast and let everything run together for a scrumptious mess.

1 cup yellow cornmeal

2 ½ cups whole milk

1 teaspoon salt

½ teaspoon garlic powder

1 ½ tablespoons melted butter

4 eggs, separated

1 teaspoon baking powder

1 cup hominy

1 jalapeño, deseeded and finely diced

1 cup grated cheese (optional)

Preheat oven to 275 degrees. Combine the cornmeal and milk in a medium saucepan and whisk until smooth. Add the salt and garlic powder. Cook over low heat until a thick mush forms. Remove from stove and stir in the melted butter, then allow to cool. Add beaten egg yolks and baking powder. Fold in stiffly beaten egg whites, hominy, and jalapeño. Spoon into a buttered casserole dish and smooth out the surface. Bake for 30 minutes.

TENNESSEE TARTE FLAMBÉE

MAKES 2 (8-INCH) PIZZAS

I WAS RAISED TO BE NO STRANGER TO "PIES" THANKS TO PHILA, but didn't start delving into savory variations until after I'd taken over Hachland Hill. Our overnight guests occasionally check in late in the evening after a long journey when they've lost all desire to explore Nashville's restaurant scene. A four-course plated meal in our dining room would be a bit much for these tired travelers, which is what prompted me to have a flavor-filled arsenal of "pies" in our freezer ready to bake for our weary guests whenever they arrive. Or, a few eggs baked on top make this one heck of a breakfast pizza!

FOR THE DOUGH:

¾ cup bread flour

½ cup water

½ teaspoon fresh yeast

1 ¼ teaspoons salt

Olive oil for the bowl

FOR THE TART:

4 ½ ounces smoked bacon, diced

2 yellow onions, thinly sliced

½ cup fromage blanc (I prefer Vermont Creamery but you may substitute cottage cheese)

½ cup crème fraiche (I prefer Grand Reserve)

1 egg

1 pinch salt

1 pinch nutmeg

1 pinch pepper

1 pinch thyme

Yellow cornmeal, for sprinkling

2 ½ ounces black truffle cheddar gruyere cheese, grated (I prefer Wood River Creamery)

Agretti, to garnish

Shaved Parmesan, to garnish

MAKE THE DOUGH: Combine the flour, water, yeast, and salt in a bowl by using your finger tips or a bench scraper. Mix until the dough just comes together. Turn the dough out onto a lightly floured surface and knead until smooth and elastic (about 5 minutes). Lightly oil a bowl with the olive oil and transfer dough to bowl, gently rubbing just a tad of oil on top to prevent it from getting crusty. Cover with plastic wrap and let it bulk ferment for 1 hour.

(continued on next page)

TENNESSEE TARTE FLAMBÉE

(*continued from previous page*)

Remove the dough from the bowl and fold it onto a work surface and let it rest for 15 minutes loosely tented with plastic wrap. Divide the dough into 2 equal pieces and shape them into rounds, then proof for 90 minutes. (The dough rounds can be individually wrapped with plastic wrap and refrigerated for 1 day or frozen for 1 month.)

MAKE THE FILLING: Place a heavy skillet over low heat and add the bacon; sauté until browned and the fat has rendered. Use a slotted spoon to transfer the bacon to a paper towel-lined plate. Add the onions to the skillet with the rendered fat over very low heat and caramelize for 1 to 2 hours. Meanwhile, in a bowl, whisk together the fromage blanc, crème fraiche, and egg. Season with the salt, nutmeg, pepper, and thyme, then set aside.

MAKE THE PIES: Preheat oven to 500 degrees. Stretch or toss your dough rounds to create two discs about 8-inches in diameter. Place each on a pizza stone or tray that has been sprinkled with cornmeal. Spoon the cream mixture onto the dough and spread to evenly disperse it within the edges of the crust. Sprinkle the bacon and caramelized onions evenly over the crusts. Top with the grated cheese and bake for 6 minutes until the tops are golden and the bottoms are browned. (Check the bottoms to ensure they're cooked through.) Remove from oven and let rest for a few minutes to allow the topping to take hold. Garnish with agretti and shaved parmesan.

Chapter 5

PIES &
OTHER SWEETS

Phila's Story
PART 5

PHILA WELCOMED HER FIRST GRANDCHILD, my brother Joseph, in 1991, followed shortly after by me in 1993, and our little sister, Liza, in 1996. She wrote *Global Feasting Tennessee Style* to celebrate the state's 200th birthday in 1996, and she dedicated it to her grandchildren and the greater youth of future generations.

In 2005, Phila moved to Joelton where she started two other business ventures with my dad. Both venues ran simultaneously for a number of years, but the original Hachland Hill in Clarksville was sold in 2001. Today, Hachland Hill is in Joelton with me as its newfound and modish patriarch carrying Phila's life torch onward. Its Main Inn, Spring Creek Inn, and 150-year-old Tobacco Barn are her lasting legacy. She told me that she was at home in Joelton. Clarksville was home too, but not the same way that Joelton was for her.

There is no one category that defines the new Hachland Hill as it plays host to so many different types of occasions and guests. The Main Inn is a bed-and-breakfast with farm-to-table dining by appointment that is open to overnight guests and the general public. Together, the Main Inn and Spring

LEFT: *Phila with her beloved grandchildren*
RIGHT: *Carter and Joseph Hach cooking on the counter at Hachland Hill*

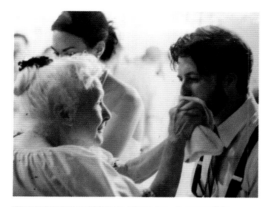

TOP LEFT: *Phila taking care of a groom*
TOP RIGHT: *Couple Amanda and Dan Howard with Phila*
BOTTOM LEFT: *Phila plating her famous wedding cake*
BOTTOM RIGHT: *One of Phila's grand wedding cakes*

Creek Inn facilitate all kinds of corporate and creative retreats with their attendees nourished by nature and the ability to enjoy all of the inclusive amenities and meals during their stay. The Tobacco Barn and its creek-side stage, surrounded by wooded hills of hiking trails and meadows, make the perfect destination wedding venue or the site for a remote concert.

As the host at Hachland Hill, Phila basked in the ambience of matrimonial occasions. Each wedding was a knock at her door, new experiences with new friends ready to answer their own door's knock with two simple words, "I do."

"Those words mark the beginning of something that is anything but simple, but everything under the sun and once the lights go out, everything when a child is born and everything when that child grows up, everything after dark hair has gone gray and smooth skin has furrowed," Phila let on with her sagacity. "When these young couples kiss and say those words, I envision the rest of their lives together. Everything at the beginning and everything at the end, that's matrimony, and matrimony is a magical thing that I've been fortunate enough to witness so many times."

Watching love ensue, like cooking, Phila told me, is one of the greatest thrills to revel in and share with others. Over the course of her career, she reckoned she had a hand in more than 500 weddings, but she bet it was closer to 1,000. She said, like apple cider vinegar and spices in a sauce, sometimes two hearts just need a firm whisking to become one. I encounter bliss in those same feelings with every overnight guest, retreat group, and bride and groom we host, and I strive to make every moment special enough so that any present hearts' flavor of love does not dilute on my watch.

Head to toe, always in her patchwork quilted apron and Birkenstock sandals with her white hair in a bun and eyebrows drawn high, Phila had a worldly innkeeper's grace that transcended guests' expectations and cultural perceptions, as rich as the Southern fare for which she was famed. She earnestly let on that she had eclectic friends all over the world, that someone could pick a city anywhere, and she had a friend there. "We're human beings to human beings, not culture to culture. You can't bridge anybody's culture," she said.

"I have an open door in my life right now, I always have.
And if somebody walks in my door and comes over, I let them into my life,"
Phila said. "And they come in easily because I have no barriers."

In June 2012, which Phila referred to as the most powerful summer she had lived, her "open door" welcomed three Middle Eastern refugee women from Nashville's International Center for Employment (NICE). "I have an open door in my life right now, I always have. And if somebody walks in my door and comes over, I let them into my life," she said. "And they come in easily because I have no barriers."

This program was meant to create a hospitality training program for refugees and immigrants. Mark Eatherly, who was the director of Refugee Integration for NICE at the time, and an attendee of most of that summer's dinners, said it was an experiment that turned into something more because of Phila.

"It was a unique moment in time," said Eatherly. "And it was what led me to want to pay homage to her with the [Phila] awards."

Eatherly created an awards event called the Philas, which is now part of an annual weeklong series of events called Fare4All. The first annual Phila Awards took place in October 2018 at Cabana, which is one of many notable Nashville restaurants started by restaurateur Randy Rayburn, who chaired the inaugural awards event that year. Rayburn coincidentally had his rehearsal dinner at Hachland Hill in Clarksville, and knew Phila to be a very special person from his time visiting there. Sow Good, the incubator that works to improve Nashville's civic and social systems for everyone's benefit, is Eatherly's associated nonprofit responsible for Fare4All and its subsidiaries. The Phila Awards were implemented to honor those who use food and cooking for virtuous purposes in Nashville. Their focus is on raising money, public support, and political will to implement a comprehensive plan to address food insecurity throughout Nashville and Davidson County.

NICE worked with a group of Vanderbilt University students to put on the hospitality training program. The students ferried the refugee women to and from Hachland Hill each week. Gity Esfahani, a former member of the Iranian air force, Siham Abdulazeez of Iraq, and Najat Al Zahawi of Kurdistan spent their Sundays in Phila's kitchen at Spring Creek, learning the ins and outs of the food business in hopes of developing businesses of their own, such as a catering company, food truck, or cooking school. Each meal was led by a different person, who would send a menu to Phila who would then buy and provide all of the ingredients for them to create that menu together. Phila always prepared a traditional Southern dish of her own to complement the other women's menus.

Eatherly fondly remembers standing in a circle and holding hands with everyone before each meal. At each day's end, upon Phila's suggestion for all of them to offer up a prayer to their respective gods, the four women held hands and one by one spoke in various languages. Reaping the fruits of their labor in a beautiful bond, they shared her table and conversed in great depth on topics ranging from food to lost loved ones. Zahawi, who told of her husband's untimely death ten years past her time in the kitchen with these women, was comforted by Phila's compassion from when she endured the same misfortune some 27 years before that summer. One year later, Zahawi taught her first cooking class at The Skillery in Nashville for the inaugural class of a series called Culture Kitchen.

"I wanted to know their culture as they wanted to know mine, but that didn't mean we have to bridge them, so we didn't," Phila said. "Those days, we were just women cooking together."

In July of 2014, Phila was diagnosed with stage 4 colon cancer and given no more than two months to live if she opted against undergoing chemotherapy. Dr. Emily Chan, associate professor of medicine and a colon cancer expert at Vanderbilt-Ingram Cancer Center, explained this was an advanced colon cancer that had already spread to her liver. Upon Chan's suggestion, and with our family's full support, she underwent chemotherapy at VICC. Chan said fit elderly patients should not be denied chemo. At the appointment when she received the grim news, Phila's response was a cheery "Marvelous!" My dad, who endured more loss than most do so early in life with his big brother and father, leaned over to ask if she heard what the doctors said to her. At this point in life, Phila certainly was hard of hearing, but she knew exactly what she was being told, and she couldn't have cared less.

"I thought, 'well, here I'm going to have an experience for two months that I've never had the opportunity for.' It wasn't about me, it was about learning about cancer," Phila said. "I never thought about me dying in two months. The hell with it, what's the difference between two months and

LEFT: *Phila during her colon cancer journey*
RIGHT: *She always brought a sense of wonder and curiosity to the experience.*

two weeks when you're 89 years old? The little innocent children here with me at the hospital have it right: Go ahead and play, and live through it."

Aside from professional courtesies, Rudy Caduff enjoyed growing his relationship with Phila through life's dealings during the 35 years that they knew one another. He explained to me how they even got a little closer at that time. He had recently gotten a lung transplant, and she called him every week when he was in the hospital.

"I thought, 'well, here I'm going to have an experience for two months that I've never had the opportunity for.' It wasn't about me, it was about learning about cancer," Phila said.

"We became even closer friends from personal experiences of something unbelievable and unreal," Rudy said at the time. "She's always so positive. She always sees something good in anything. It can be the worst thing happening, and she sees something good about it. That's Phila, she is something."

Each fall, the Fertel Foundation pays homage to an unsung hero in the Southern food family. In 2015, they commemorated a Tennessee trailblazer of down-home cooking culture, the culinary queen and my grandmother, Phila. On October 16, at the 18th Southern Foodways Symposium in Oxford, Mississippi, Joe Hach accepted the Ruth Fertel Keeper of the Flame Award on his mother's behalf.

Randy Fertel, son of Ruth Fertel for whom the award was named, delivered a warm welcome to my dad and me at the event. Ruth Fertel is the late proprietor of widely known Ruth's Chris Steakhouse. Since serving as a busboy, a manager and the director of marketing for his mother's restaurant conglomerate, Randy received a PhD from Harvard University and has been steadfast in the food industry, cultivating a reputable writing career. Randy is president of both the Fertel Foundation and the Ruth U. Fertel Foundation.

In a short film interviewing Phila for the ceremony, she spoke about life being a multitude of moments.

Afterward, Randy Fertel spoke to the audience. "I've been in love with Phila Hach since I saw a picture of her biscuits on a website that honors her. I love that her first name means love. I love, too, that the site says that a key ingredient in Hach's recipe for success is 'Remaining open to the moment.' This is a theme Mrs. Hach shares with all the improvisers I've written about in my new book, *Forgive Me The Plug*, but more importantly she shares it with my mother," he said. "Mom, I like to say, was an accidental entrepreneur, an accidental empress. She didn't start out to build an empire of steak houses but just kept building as opportunities presented. I love Mrs. Hach's saying, 'Time is a multitude of moments: I have let my moments empower my life.' I recently heard the world broken into two types, the sledgehammers and the hummingbirds, not unlike Isaiah Berlin's idea of the hedgehogs and foxes: 'The fox knows many things, but the hedgehog knows one big thing.' The first, like my mother, the sledgehammering hedgehog burrows into one thing and never lets go. The other, like Mrs. Hach, fox or hummingbird, are more cagey and flit from interest to interest, flower to flower, airline stewardess to TV innovator to innkeeper to UN provisioner."

John T. Edge, the founding director of the Southern Foodways Alliance, spoke next. "The pioneers were people like Phila Hach, who cobbled together a career doing multiple things very well, whether that was her work with the airlines, or her work writing books, or her work in television, or her work for the World's Fair, or her work consulting," Edge said. "She blazed a path that now others follow, and it's important to remember who came before."

Phila truly lived a life unto her favorite colloquialism: Don't take any wooden nickels.

"Every time we get up in the morning, the day is already planned, the clouds are up there. It's already planned, and you can't change one thing about it. You can only reject the day if it's raining or you can absorb that rain," Phila told me during an interview that took place close to her passing. "I've learned not to reject anything, live with a free spirit and it's a fun way to live. I have to die, because that's the price of living eternally. I hope when I die that no one will ever shed a tear, because I've had the most unpredictable life. I hope no one cries ever about my demise, because I've lived it to the hill."

The Vanderbilt University Medical Center Reporter published an article, "Hach Shows Age Not Always a Barrier to Cancer Therapy," accounting her apparent progress to affirm their belief that there is a difference between chronological age and physiological age. A full year later than the two months that she was given to live in the original diagnosis, she discontinued her chemotherapy.

From humble beginnings of making mud pies to serving international dignitaries, and then two supposed months that turned into 13, Phila kept her door open to the very end and greeted every knock with vigor and a country cooking notion that knew no bounds.

Phila's door closed after 89 marvelous years in 2015, but I'm keeping the fire and food warm for her soul and for anyone who crosses the threshold of our openhearted home at Hachland Hill.

Phila Hach, Hachland Hill, 2014

SCRATCH THAT COBBLER

SERVES 10

I HAVE ALWAYS LOVED A GOOD COBBLER. Unfortunately, by the time I was invested in taking over Hachland Hill's kitchen, any notion of a scratch recipe had gone out the window in Phila's final years. Ruth presented me with a frozen blackberry cobbler purchased from the now-closed restaurant supply store known as Cash & Carry. This went against the foundation of Hachland Hill, so I said "scratch that" and began experimenting to create a cobbler that would honor Phila's gourmet legacy. This has become a very popular dessert for our songwriting retreats and those private dining guests seeking a Southern staple made the right way!

1 tablespoon cornstarch

2 tablespoons water

Juice of 1 lemon

2 cups black raspberries (or use your favorite berries)

½ cup, sugar, plus ⅓ cup for meal mixture

1 teaspoon dried thyme

1 tablespoon lemon zest

1⅔ cups all-purpose flour

½ cup blanched almonds

¼ teaspoon salt

1 tablespoon dried pineapple sage, ground

1½ sticks unsalted butter, cubed into dice-sized pieces

4 tablespoons ice-cold water
Lemon balm crème diplomat (recipe follows)

Vanilla ice cream

Citrus gem marigold & pineapple sage petals (or use rose petals)

Preheat oven to 375 degrees.

Coat a casserole dish with non-stick baking spray. Dissolve the cornstarch in the water and lemon juice. Whisk until there are no lumps. Using a rubber spatula or gloved hands, work the berries, ½ cup sugar, thyme, and lemon zest in a large bowl, then pour the cornstarch mixture over the berries and work again with a spatula or hands until evenly coated. Pour the filling into the prepared dish.

(continued on next page)

(continued from previous page)

In a food processor, combine the flour, almonds, remaining sugar, salt, pineapple sage, and butter. Blend until the mixture forms a course meal. Slowly add the cold water, drizzling through the top 1 tablespoon at a time, and pulse until a dough comes together and pulls away from the sides of the processor. Turn the dough out onto a floured counter and pat into a rectangle, then roll into a ¼-inch-thick sheet and trim it to the size of your baking dish.

Carefully transfer the sheet of dough over top of the filling and gently press it to the sides of the dish; be careful so that the filling doesn't ooze above the crust. Prick the dough in a few spots with a fork. Bake until crust is golden brown and the filling is thick, about 40 minutes. If the crust starts to get too dark, cover it with aluminum foil and continue baking until done.

Serve the cobbler with a dollop of the crème diplomat and scoop of vanilla ice cream, then garnish with the flower petals. .

LEMON BALM CRÈME DIPLOMAT

MAKES ABOUT 4 CUPS

Crème pâtissière (page 238), excluding the whiskey	1 teaspoon fresh lemon balm, finely chopped
3 cups chantilly cream (page 235)	¼ teaspoon fresh pineapple sage, finely chopped

In a stand mixer fitted with a whisk attachment, combine the cooled crème pâtissière and chantilly cream. Mix until smooth and evenly incorporated. Fold in the lemon balm and pineapple sage.

PERSIMMON OZARK PUDDING

SERVES 8

THE OZARKS, SPECIFICALLY THEIR WATERS, bring back so many memories for me. The White River, originating in the Ozark-St. Francis National Forest of the Boston Mountains, flows through Arkansas and Missouri before eventually feeding into the Mississippi River. This is where my dad would take his annual fishing trip and he eventually took me once I was of age. I was much older when I first heard of Ozark Pudding. I didn't have a clue what the dish entailed, but its name was special enough for me that I had to try it out. It is most widely known as one of former President Harry Truman's favorite foods that his wife, Bess, would prepare for him. The fruit and nut custard, as the name suggests, appears to have been fostered in the Arkansas and Missouri Ozarks. While apples, hazelnuts, or black walnuts, may have been original ingredients, like with any old recipe, the dish changed over time as people recreated it in their own vision to make it personal. I grew up eating persimmons off one of the trees behind the barn at Hachland Hill. It immediately occurred to me that those delectable little fruits from my past would be my twist on this "olde-worlde" dish.

1 egg

¾ cup sugar

2 tablespoons all-purpose flour

1 ¼ teaspoons baking powder

⅛ teaspoon salt

½ cup black walnuts, chopped

½ cup persimmons, chopped

1 teaspoon pure vanilla extract

Vanilla-coffee sauce (page 236)

Whipped cream

Preheat oven to 350 degrees. Beat the egg and sugar with a whisk until thick and reaches the color of lemon. Add the remaining ingredients and mix thoroughly until evenly incorporated. Bake in a buttered Pyrex dish for 35 minutes. To serve, spoon into a bowl and top with the vanilla-coffee sauce and whipped cream.

OLD FASHIONED TEA CAKES

MAKES 10 TO 14 CAKES

I USED TO SCARF THESE DOWN WHENEVER PHILA MADE THEM for me as a young boy. They're light, airy and tasty as all get out. I used to watch in awe as she pumped out perfect flowers of frosting from her pastry bag to garnish them. They are a wonderful dessert or sugary petit four at a dinner party.

FOR THE CAKES:

1 ½ sticks butter

2 cups sugar

2 eggs

6 cups cake flour, sifted

6 scant teaspoons baking powder

2 teaspoons nutmeg

About 1 ⅓ cups whole milk or enough to form soft dough

1 tablespoon pure vanilla extract

1 tablespoon rosewater

FOR THE GLAZE:

1 teaspoon plain gelatin

⅔ cup cold water

8 cups powdered sugar

1 egg white

1 tablespoon white corn syrup

Food coloring (optional)

MAKE THE CAKES: Preheat oven to 325 degrees. In a stand mixer fitted with a paddle attachment, cream together the butter and sugar. Add the eggs and blend thoroughly. In a separate bowl, mix and sift together the dry ingredients, then add them to the creamed mixture alternating with the milk. Add the vanilla and rosewater and mix to incorporate. Transfer to a clean bowl and let stand for 4 hours to ripen. Roll dough into 4-inch rounds and bake until light brown. Remove from oven and let cool, then wrap and freeze.

MAKE THE GLAZE: Using a double boiler, dissolve the gelatin in cold water. Add the remaining ingredients and stir until blended. Place over hot water and warm to 110 degrees (it should be warm to the touch). Dip frozen tea cakes in glaze and allow to dry. Decorate and garnish as desired.

LEBKUCHEN
(*or* DELICIOUS GERMAN CAKES)

MAKES ABOUT 16 SMALL CAKES

PHILA WAS KNOWN FOR HER COOKIES, especially around the holidays. This particular confection is something of a hybrid between spiced tea cake and a cookie. The smell and taste always remind of me of winter. Next time you have a cookie party, ditch the chocolate chips and try these for something special fit for Ole St. Nick!

1 cup molasses

1 cup honey

3 cups sugar

1 ¼ cups shortening

11 cups all-purpose flour, divided

½ cup almonds, chopped, plus more for garnish

1 ½ cup mix of walnuts and pecans, chopped

1 teaspoon cinnamon

1 teaspoon cloves

2 tablespoons brandy

½ cup citron, chopped

1 teaspoon salt

1 teaspoon baking soda

3 eggs, well beaten

1 cup powdered sugar

In a heavy-bottomed pot, bring the molasses, honey, and sugar to a boil and simmer for 5 minutes. Reduce heat but while still hot, stir in the shortening, 4 cups flour, nuts, cinnamon, cloves, brandy, citron, and salt. Let cool. Dissolve the baking soda in 1 cup boiling water then add to dough. Add the eggs one at a time, then the remaining flour as needed to make a stiff dough. Wrap in plastic wrap and refrigerate for 3 to 4 days.

Preheat oven to 350 degrees. Roll out the dough onto a floured work surface, and cut into desired shapes. Bake in the oven for 12 to 16 minutes. Make a powdered glaze by adding 2 tablespoons hot water to the powdered sugar and stir to combine. Frost the cakes with the glaze and decorate with almonds.

CLOUDY *with a* CHANCE OF FUDGE

SERVES 8

FUDGE PIE WAS ANOTHER ONE OF PHILA'S CONSTANT FAVORITES for her guests at Hachland Hill. I ditched the pie shell for a dish and the rest is history. I still do love making it as a pie whenever I'm feeling nostalgic. I remember the first time I tested it devoid of dough with my mom as a guinea pig. "This has got to be in your cookbook," she told me.

½ cup melted butter

4 whole eggs

¼ teaspoon salt

⅓ cup dark cocoa powder, sifted

1 cup sugar

1 teaspoon pure vanilla extract

Chantilly cream (page 235)

2 teaspoons raspberry liqueur

Vanilla ice cream

Fresh chocolate mint for garnish

Preheat oven to 350 degrees. Whisk all ingredients together quickly. Grease eight oven-safe ramekins with non-stick baking spray. Divide the batter evenly between ramekins, set ramekins on a baking sheet, and bake for 7 minutes, then turn the tray and continue to bake until set, about 8 minutes more (give or take depending on size of dish). Do not overcook! It should have a custard-like texture.

Let the ramekins cool slightly then carefully invert them onto a work surface, tapping them on the counter if they don't come out easy on their own.

Prepare chantilly cream according to recipe, adding raspberry liqueur when it starts to form peaks. Place a serving of fudge brownie at the center of each plate and pipe the raspberry cream on top. Add a petit quenelle of vanilla ice cream beside the brownie. Garnish with fresh mint.

PEACHY, BOOZY PECAN PIE

SERVES 8

PHILA'S PECAN PIE IS PERFECT! I adapted it slightly with peach and brandy (inspired by Phila's sister and niece) but take those away, and there you have her classic recipe.

FOR THE PIE:

3 eggs

1 teaspoon vanilla

2 tablespoons peach brandy

3 tablespoons melted butter

½ teaspoon salt

½ cup sugar

1 cup dark karo syrup

1 unbaked foolproof pie crust (page 178)

Pinch of cornstarch

1 large peach, peeled and sliced thin

¾ cup pecans, chopped

¼ cup pecans, whole

FOR THE CRÈME DIPLOMAT:

Peach whiskey crème pâtissière (page 238)

3 cups chantilly cream (page 235)

MAKE THE FILLING: Preheat oven to 375 degrees. Beat eggs slightly. Add vanilla, brandy, butter, salt, sugar, and karo syrup. Whisk vigorously until mixture is very smooth. Dust pie shell with cornstarch and rub to evenly coat its bottom and sides, staying off the rim. Invert the pan to shake off any excess cornstarch. Layer the sliced peaches in the bottom of the pie crust but keep them from overlapping. Evenly disperse the pecans on top of the peach slices, then pour the filling over the pecans and watch as they rise to the surface. Carefully set the pie on a sheet tray and place in the oven to bake for 12 minutes; reduce heat to 325 degrees, rotate tray, and continue baking until pie is set.

MAKE THE CRÈME DIPLOMAT: In a stand mixer fitted with a whisk attachment, combine the crème pâtissière and chantilly cream. Mix until smooth and evenly incorporated. Spoon onto a warm slice of pie.

LEMON BASIL CHESS PIE

SERVES 8

CHESS PIE IS A MYSTERY TO ANYONE OUTSIDE OF THE SOUTH, though it did experience a renaissance of sorts when renowned baker Christina Tosi introduced it to New York while working for chef David Chang. She dubbed her miso-infused version "crack pie." She went on to found the iconic Milk Bar confectionary empire. Chess pie originally got its name because the traditional crust was made from milled chestnuts. I find great joy in introducing our out-of-town guests to this sugary Southern secret.

1 stick butter

1 cup sugar

3 eggs

2 teaspoons lemon zest

1 teaspoon pure vanilla extract

1 teaspoon almond extract

1 teaspoon dried lemon basil, ground

1 unbaked foolproof pie crust (page 178)

1 tablespoon yellow cornmeal

Preheat oven to 400 degrees. In a stand mixer fitted with a paddle attachment, cream the butter; add sugar gradually and blend thoroughly. (It may be necessary to scrape the bottom and sides of the bowl.) Add the eggs and beat well. Mix in the lemon zest, vanilla and almond extracts, and lemon basil. Sprinkle the unbaked pie shell with the cornmeal, then pour in the pie filling. Bake for 12 minutes. Reduce the temperature to 350 degrees, rotate the pie, and bake for 15 minutes longer until done.

OLD FASHIONED CARAMEL PIE

SERVES 8

CARAMEL PIE IS ONE OF THOSE DESSERTS that hasn't yet seen its day in the sun on restaurant menus, even at meat-and-threes, but I strive to give it the attention it deserves by including it in this book. I stole a page from pastry chef Christina Tosi and added a little umami to Phila's recipe, giving it a novel gastronomic element, which everyone seems to crave today.

1 ¼ cups sugar, divided, plus 6 tablespoons for the meringue

2 tablespoons all-purpose flour

1 tablespoon cornstarch

Dash of salt

⅛ teaspoon miso powder

2 tablespoons melted butter

1 ½ cups sweetened condensed milk

3 eggs, separated

1 baked foolproof pie crust (page 178)

Preheat oven to 300 degrees. In a heavy skillet, heat ¼ cup sugar over medium heat to caramelize it. *Do not* stir. While the sugar is caramelizing, in a saucepan, combine the remaining sugar, flour, cornstarch, salt, and miso powder with the butter and milk. Blend in the egg yolks and cook over low heat until thick. Add the hot caramel sugar to the custard and stir until smooth, then continue to cook until thick and creamy. Pour mixture into prepared pie crust. Make a meringue from the egg whites and 6 tablespoons sugar; top the pie with the meringue. Heat in oven until just browned, then remove and let cool before serving.

PEANUT BUTTER-FUDGE PIE

SERVES 8

IN ONE OF MY FIRST WEDDING SEASONS leading the kitchen at Hachland Hill, we had a bride with a penchant for chocolate and peanut butter. I remember thinking, "that is one lucky groom marrying a girl with that palate." (I gravitate toward the Reese's whenever I find myself perusing junk food at a gas station. My wife, who inherently favors savory over sweet, still revels in the riches of Reese's with me when we're on the road, which is just one small-cup-sized reason why I am the luckiest husband in candyland.) I combined Phila's fudge pie and peanut butter pie recipes to create this dessert for the couple's rehearsal dinner. It's not every day that you see a pie referenced as a highlight of a wedding venue, but this bride's review on theKnot.com did just that for Hachland Hill. Their sugar-fueled smiles the night before their wedding are a delightful memory, and I treasure those little moments with my clients as they begin the rest of their lives together.

FOR THE PEANUT BUTTER FILLING:

4 eggs

1 ¼ cups sugar

¼ cup melted butter

1 cup sour cream

½ cup peanut butter

1 tablespoon pure vanilla extract

1 unbaked foolproof pie crust (page 178)

FOR THE FUDGE FILLING:

½ cup melted butter

4 whole eggs

¼ teaspoon salt

⅓ cup cocoa powder, sifted

1 cup sugar

1 teaspoon pure vanilla extract

MAKE THE PEANUT BUTTER FILLING: Preheat oven to 350 degrees. Mix together eggs, sugar, butter, sour cream, peanut butter, and vanilla until smooth and evenly incorporated. Pour into pie shell until it fills the crust halfway and set aside.

MAKE THE FUDGE FILLING: Mix all ingredients together until smooth and evenly incorporated. Slowly pour into the center of the peanut butter filling until it fills the shell. Bake for 35 minutes, turning once.

FOGGY COCONUT CAKE

SERVES 10 TO 14

I REMEMBER ONE TIME, in Phila's later years when her sureness had become a little foggy, she took her belief in country cooking a bit too far. She did always say that country cooking was using whatever was available, and she certainly practiced what she preached in this particular instance. She had our family and a small collective of her closest friends out for a lunch at Hachland Hill's Spring Creek Inn. Coconut cake was to be the dessert. We often had a slice of it along with boiled custard around the holidays. Her cake, or dessert in general, was usually the rock star of her menus. No one, who was there to try that cake, would ever forget it—but this time for another reason. Upon realizing that her coconut shavings had run out, she quickly made use of some beautiful white bars of soap that were grated atop her cake to finish it. That was her country cooking, but I think we all would have been just fine without the inventive garnish that day.

FOR THE CAKE:

3 cups cake flour, sifted

2 teaspoons baking powder

¼ teaspoon salt

1 cup butter

3 ½ cups powdered sugar

4 egg yolks, beaten well

1 cup whole milk

1 teaspoon pure vanilla extract

1 cup fresh grated coconut, plus more for garnish

4 egg whites, beaten stiff

¾ cup fresh coconut milk

Food coloring to tint the batter (optional)

FOR THE FLUFFY FROSTING:

3 egg whites, unbeaten

½ cup water

2 ¼ cups sugar

2 teaspoons corn syrup

1 ½ teaspoons vanilla

(continued on next page)

FOGGY COCONUT CAKE

(continued from previous page)

MAKE THE CAKE: Preheat oven to 350 degrees. Combine the sifted cake flour, baking powder, and salt, and sift together three times. In a stand mixer fitted with a paddle attachment, cream the butter and sugar until fluffy. Add the egg yolk and beat for 2 minutes. Add the flour mixture alternating with the milk, stirring after each addition, then add the vanilla and coconut. Fold in the stiffly beaten egg whites. Coat three 9-inch cake pans with nonstick baking spray and fill each with equal amounts batter. Bake for 25 to 35 minutes or until done. Let the layers cool, then remove from pans and drizzle their tops with the coconut milk.

MAKE THE FROSTING: Place egg whites, water, sugar, corn syrup, and vanilla in a double boiler. Cook and beat for 7 minutes until fluffy and forms stiff peaks.

Assemble cake into three tiers. Ice cake with the frosting and sprinkle with additional grated coconut.

TIRAMISU CRÈME BRÛLÉE

MAKES ABOUT 8 SERVINGS

I LIKE MAKING DIFFERENT VARIATIONS OF CRÈME BRÛLÉE for our fancier dinner parties at Hachland Hill. For one rehearsal dinner I did, the couple requested an Italian menu with my farm-to-table influence. Their meal consisted of a salad, an assortment of pizzas and pastas, and this decadent version of crème brûlée. It is one of those desserts that makes the dining room go quiet!

8 lady finger cookies

2 cups strong coffee, chilled

2 tablespoons cocoa powder

18 duck egg yolks

1 ¾ cups sugar

1 vanilla bean, fileted and scraped

5 cups heavy cream

½ cup cypress needles (kept intact)

8 tablespoons light brown sugar

Special equipment: 8 soufflé dishes or custard cups

Preheat oven to 350 degrees.

Place soufflé dishes or custard cups in large roasting pan. Submerge lady fingers in coffee for 8 minutes. Remove lady fingers and gently pat them dry, then cut them in half crosswise and rest the two pieces side-by-side in the bottom of each soufflé dish. Sprinkle each with cocoa powder.

In a large bowl, whisk together the egg yolks, sugar, and vanilla bean meat until the mixture becomes pale yellow. In a heavy saucepan, bring cream and cypress needles to a boil. Once boiling, remove the needles with a slotted spoon and discard. Gradually whisk the hot cream into the egg yolk mixture.

Pour custard into soufflé dishes, dividing equally among them. Pour enough hot water into the roasting pan to come halfway up the sides of the soufflé dishes. Bake custards until just set in their centers, about 30 minutes. Remove dishes from water and let cool completely. Cover and refrigerate for at least 6 hours. Sprinkle 1 tablespoon brown sugar over each dish and torch with a blowtorch, or place dishes in a roasting pan and broil until the sugar melts and turns dark brown, about 2 minutes.

PHILA'S FAMOUS BUTTER CAKE

SERVES 16

PHILA USED TO REGULARLY SERVE THIS at Hachland Hill in Clarksville. It was an invention of hers that I have not messed with to this day, because it hits all of the notes that she set out for it to satisfy the guests. This was Phila's idea for an amusing treat that could achieve the same end as the flaming Bananas Foster to her guests, but with ingredients that were always handy in her pantry.

2 sticks butter	1 cup whole milk
2 cups sugar	1 teaspoon vanilla
2 ½ teaspoons baking powder	Ice cream
⅛ teaspoon salt	Whipped cream
3 cups cake flour, sifted	Brandy sugar
5 eggs, separated	

Preheat oven to 350 degrees. In a stand mixer with fitted with a paddle attachment, cream the butter and sugar until light. Add the baking powder and salt to the sifted cake flour, then sift all together once more. Add the dry ingredients to the mixing bowl, alternating with the egg yolks and milk, mixing after each addition. Add the vanilla and combine. Beat the egg whites, then fold in to batter. Coat two 12-inch cake pans with nonstick cooking spray, then fill with equal amounts batter and bake for 40 minutes. Split each warm cake into two layers. For each cake, between each layer, spread your favorite ice cream. Place the top layers over the ice cream and press firmly. Ice the cakes all over with whipped cream. Dash a spoonful of brandy sugar on top, set aflame and send to the table flambé.

WEDDING CAKE

SERVES 8

IT'D BE SIN, AS THE PROPRIETOR OF A WEDDING VENUE, to not share a wedding cake recipe in this book. Phila always inspired me when she would decorate her cakes for display at Hachland Hill weddings back in Clarksville. I caught the bug and studied cakes in New York with Jurgen David and Kieran Baldwin at the ICC in honor of Phila's craft, which mesmerized me as a young boy. Read the comical story of when I first fell in love with cake on page 223—it had everyone involved on the edge of their seats!

FOR THE WHITE CAKE:

2 sticks butter

2 ½ cups sugar

½ teaspoon pure vanilla extract

½ teaspoon lemon extract

9 egg whites

½ teaspoon baking powder

1 ½ teaspoons cream of tartar

4 cups cake flour, sifted

1 cup buttermilk

½ teaspoon baking soda

SWISS MERINGUE BUTTERCREAM:

¾ cup pasteurized egg whites

1 ½ cups sugar

4 sticks unsalted butter, cut into cubes

1 cup praline paste

TO ASSEMBLE:

Jam or cream for filling (your choice)

(continued on next page)

(continued from previous page)

MAKE THE WHITE CAKE: Preheat oven to 350 degrees. In a stand mixer fitted with a paddle attachment, cream the butter, sugar, and flavorings together. Add the egg whites one at a time with the mixer running, beating hard to fully incorporate in between each white. Sift the baking powder and cream of tartar together with the already once sifted cake flour. Add the dry ingredients to the mixing bowl, alternating with the buttermilk. Add baking soda to the last ¼ cup of buttermilk. Finish by adding the dry mix last. Coat two 9-inch cake pans with non-stick spray and fill with batter. Bake for 35 to 40 minutes or until done. Let cool then remove cake from pans.

MAKE THE BUTTERCREAM: In the bowl of a stand mixer fitted with a whisk attachment, lightly whisk the egg whites and sugar together, then place the bowl over a pot of simmering water (be sure the bottom isn't touching the water). Lightly whisk the mixture by hand over the simmering water until the mixture is hot to the touch. Return the bowl to the mixer and whip on medium-high speed until doubled in volume. Whisk until the meringue reaches medium to stiff peaks and has cooled down. Replace the whisk with the paddle attachment and add the butter to the meringue a few pieces at a time with the mixer running, until all of the butter is incorporated. Increase the speed and beat until the buttercream is light and fluffy. Fold the praline paste into the butter cream with a rubber spatula until evenly incorporated.

TO ASSEMBLE: Pipe your favorite filling of jam or cream in between the cake layers and ice with the buttercream using an offset spatula and bench scraper.

THE GREAT WEDDING CAKE HEIST

I had a proclivity for sweets, especially cake, from a very young age. (I want you to close your eyes and envision a set of feeble hands caressing a pastry bag, meticulously decorating with pastel-colored icing, so as to make every flower perfect.)

But one particular cake stands out, and that was Phila's wedding cake. On the day of the event, guests arrived early, on time, casually late, and rudely past any norm, occasionally walking through the foyer into the garden room to marvel over the picturesque five-tier wedding cake. Supported only by fleshed flowers, daring to withstand the use of gaudy but safe pillars, the base's diameter diminished as each layer climbed to the top. Rolled fondant, sugary and pliable, coated the exterior giving a proper surface to sow roses. The inside, as fine and white as the bride's veil, was dreamily light and moist with a marzipan maze burrowing throughout it to create unmapped caverns of sudden almond flavor.

The top layer swayed above its subjects with a bride and groom figurine trembling at the rap of guests' shoes shaking the floor below the table. The garden room was a sight to behold. Its floor was on par with an Augusta green and its wall, one giant sheet of glass, looked onto a majestic flora of exotic plants and a pond with exquisitely carved stone angels standing guard. The glossy water mirrored the green violet-ear hummingbirds doing courtship dives and buzzing their vibrating wings.

There is no telling how much time was spent on the cake's preparation. It very well could have been an extraordinary amount of time, only there was no telling an embellishment from a white lie, from a slight truth, from a fact, when you asked Phifee. She loved her own legend as it grew. (My wife, Amber, has joked with my dad and peers that I inherited my humility from my grandmother.) Phifee claimed the masterpiece took no more than fifteen minutes of prep time, aside from the baking of course. Wit aside, the cake was artistry at its finest.

People dissipated from the garden room into the awe-inspiring ballroom, where ceilings were high, chandeliers were precious, and hardwoods were waxy slick for the reception. The staff was in high gear, half running drinks and half clearing plates, while sweltering line cooks prepared one course after the next. The mature eyes of Phifee, occasionally popping in to check the cake's stature, and the hummingbirds with their unvarying buzz on the other side of the glass were all that laid claim to the unmanned cake. Wedged into one of the room's corners, the table veiled a blind spot between its linens and the wall. If someone looked closely, they could have spotted two pairs of little feet poking out from the drapery, one in boots and the other in sneakers. I wore my cowboy boots everywhere I went as a youngster.

Unbeknownst to anyone and everything but the birds, Joseph and I snuck

(continued on next page)

(continued from previous page)

underneath there when the guests made the switch to the ballroom. Earlier, when everyone was in the garden room, so enamored by the cake, we snuck about the ballroom to steal a bowl of olives off the bar that we brought with us to fill up on under the table. They exited out of one door, and we scurried through another. We were told to stay upstairs and play in our dad's old room, but that was asking a whole lot of us. Shoot, we were boys, five and seven years old, spending the night at a hotel during a wedding.

The first and last course came and went, devoured on sight, until all of the plates were cleared and back in the kitchen for washing. Despite newborn food babies, tummies growled at every table in eager anticipation of their slice, and lazy mouths aggressively guzzled champagne with a drunk munchy desire forming in their soon to be frosting-filled cheeks. Phifee, observing her well-served guests with literally and figuratively raised spirits, paced into the garden room for the cake's final inspection before its risky transfer to the ballroom. With a sharp left through the doorframe, she faced the table to find a cloth that boasted gifts galore, accompanying nosh plates of white delight, and the safe and sound cake. All was well and how she'd left it—all but the absentee top layer with its cold footed bride and groom. Flabbergasted to the point of being mute, her mouth sanctioned none of the syllables she sought to shout but her insides screamed to high heavens for Miss Ruth and Miss Sally. If she mustered her bark, Joseph and I may have been scared

into lifting up the tablecloth and giving up our treasure.

Phifee, scolding the staff, ordered them to retrieve the cake's base at once and roll it to the kitchen as stealthily and speedily as possible to avoid visibility from the ballroom. She was hard at work, hoping to crank out another top layer before anyone noticed the missing original. The head bridesmaid arrived to the garden room and freaked out upon her discovery, saving no syllables for herself. She faced the table to find a cloth that boasted gifts galore and accompanying nosh plates of white delight, and only a top layer of the cake with its bride and groom toppers ready for wedlock.

All was well and how she'd left it—all but the vanished four layers that the top layer had once graced. She exploded through the kitchen's forest green door swinging in response, feistily fussing at Phifee who focused on the cake and paid the woman no mind. Phifee said of the incident, "I heard that shrill voice boom from the garden room, 'Where on God's green earth is that cake. Ugh.' And just in the nick of time, I was able to shield the replacement top layer that was being coated with fondant."

Phifee said, "Don't worry, dearie. I'm just tending to some last-minute touches." She dreaded the inevitable question, "And the top layer?" said in a perfect medium between soft and snarky.

Worried her gambit had run its course, Phifee set the pastry bag on the counter beside her and slowly looked up to confidently answer, "Yes, dearie, I'm taking care of that too."

Pies & Other Sweets

WEDDING CAKE

"Don't mind that. It looks perfect. Let's bring it in. You're an angel, Miss Phila," said the cheerily unsettling voice of a head bridesmaid, who then headed out the still swinging door.

I'm still surprised we didn't at least try to put a dent in it, but those olives had stuffed us to the point of clammy foreheads and watery joules. We didn't know the dangers of boozy olives.

An unexpected event unraveled, raising questions about the cake's past. Phifee arrived back to the garden room with the bulk of the cake, scratching her white bun, facing the table to find a cloth that now boasted gifting galore and accompanying nosh plates of white delight. All was well and how she'd left it—the top layer with its cold footed bride and groom had runoff yet again. There was no cake in sight besides the bottom four layers on the cart that she steered with tightly clinched fists in wake of a disheveled corner of the tablecloth shedding light on a pair of boots and sneakers.

Waxy slick floors make for the superb sliding, which is why Joseph and I only ever wore our socks in the ballroom. Phifee was well aware of this routine of ours.

For whatever reason, maybe being a few years my senior, Joseph had the sense to abandon ship. The stakes were clearly higher with an audience, especially when we had been ordered to avoid the ball room and its guests. I didn't share the same consciousness as my big brother that day. I was the cutest kid, I knew this, and I wasn't done with my performance. My inherent humility that Amber jokes about was there from the beginning. I started with the top

layer, hoisted above my barely sustaining shoulders, marching to my attempt at a classic wedding verse, "Here comes the bride. All step aside. Dn, dn, dn, dn, dn... Here comes the bride. All step aside for the pretty bride." With my fingers indenting its sides, I nailed a textbook sock slide and came to a halt at the bride and groom's table. Phifee appeared in a panic at the doorway where a proud Joseph was spectating. Hands cupped on her flushed cheeks, wrestling with the decision to spank Joseph then or wait until she had me too, she watched my finale pan out since the damage had been done.

We were shown mercy thanks to the bride finding me as cute as a button. Better than that, a real godsend, she hunched over and kissed me on the forehead.

I reckon that maid-of-honor was ready to drown me in the pond outside of the garden room. My dad, much to my mom's chagrin, was thrown in there on his wedding night by my cousin Ned. Mama never let Ned live that one down.

We pulled off the wedding cake heist, knowing our slightest bump of the table would have offset the cake into a collapse capable of ruining the night altogether. Phifee's mind was truly blown away by our managing to avoid contact down there, and moreover amazed that I transported it bar-back style to the ballroom without a single portion plummeting. Cooking was in our blood, and we played a most important part on this most special day, making our grandma proud to have grandsons so adept at her career. Some things are a piece of cake when you're having fun doing them.

———————

Chapter 6

———————

LARDER

Phila's Story

PART 6

ONE OF MY MOST VIVID CHILDHOOD MEMORIES is sitting on the marble counter in the kitchen at Hachland Hill with my brother, Joseph, and sister, Liza. Whenever our parents deservedly needed a break from us and our antics, they'd make the hour-long trek to Clarksville and hand us off to Phila so that they could enjoy the peace and quiet of an empty nest back home in Nashville for a weekend. The marble counter was our sauce station, as we still call it, and it was where we worked while Phila tended to the stove nearby. Our sauce station was Phila's larder. Her office, riddled with photos of her former guests and friends scotch-taped on every surface, was just on the other side of the wall from the kitchen. It was a mess of an office with gardening tools, pages of handwritten recipes, dog beds, and scrolls from an ancient typewriter covering a floor that I don't recall ever seeing.

There was a window beside her desk, that swung open between the stove and our sauce station, which allowed Phila to leisurely peek into the kitchen as she kept a close eye on her cooks—we were likely the paramount worry.

The sauce station's counter was cold on my bottom. I can still feel the chill. It was where she had all of her spices and intimidating mixers. Phila always warned us of the Hobart mixer's danger with constant reminders that we could get our little arms chopped off by it. It was massive sitting next to us on the counter. I still have it today at Hachland Hill, and while I don't fear that a part of me will be chopped off by it now, I do know better than to go for a finger dab of frosting while it is running!

During those visits, we blended obscure spices with no rhyme or reason, giving rise to our special sauces with hints of everything—the works, the kitchen sink. Watching our hands so as not to lose limbs, we'd shake jars and bottles until a thickness emerged, a concoction of sweet, sour, salty, sugary spicy, tangy, bitter, bland, and any other flavor. We whisked

TOP: *Carter (left) and Joseph making a concoction at the sauce station*
BOTTOM: *The boys "helping" Phila at Hachland Hill*

as vigorously as our little hands would allow. We watched in awe of Phila, in the same way that she had viewed the pastry chef at the hotel in Chattanooga, and this was where we learned to cook with no recipes. This was our chapter one of country cooking.

"Joseph and Carter, my wonderfully wild grandsons, sat on that counter whenever they could," Phila said. "Their little legs dangled down and they banged their little boots on those cabinets, carrying on and making sauces. They'd throw in anything and everything. And let me tell you, it was fabulous. It was country cooking."

MAYONNAISE

MAKES 2 ¼ CUPS

2 egg yolks, at room temperature

1 teaspoon fine salt

1 teaspoon dry ground mustard seed

4 pinches sugar

½ teaspoon cayenne pepper

4 teaspoons freshly squeezed lemon juice

2 tablespoons champagne vinegar

2 cups corn oil

In a food processor, pulse together the yolks, salt, mustard seed, sugar, and cayenne. In a separate bowl, combine lemon juice and vinegar; add half of the lemon juice mixture to the yolk mixture. While machine is running, slowly add oil through the top of the processor one drop at a time until it has thickened and lightened to a pale-yellow emulsion. Increase your oil flow to a thin stream until half of it is evenly incorporated. Add the remaining lemon juice mixture. Continue blending and drizzle in the rest of the oil until combined. (You may need to scrape the sides of the bowl with a rubber spatula a few times between blending to ensure there are no more lumps.) Scrape mixture into a bowl and let sit at room temperature for 1 hour. Seal in an airtight container for up to one week.

MINT AÏOLI

MAKES 2 ½ CUPS

2 cups mayonnaise (see above or it better be Duke's)

½ cup fresh mint, coarsely chopped

6 garlic cloves, minced

2 teaspoons grated lemon rind

½ teaspoon smoked paprika

1 teaspoon salt

1 teaspoon black pepper

3 tablespoons fresh lemon juice

Blend all ingredients together in a food processor. Continue to pulse, stopping to scrape down the bottom and sides, until aïoli is smooth and creamy.

LEMON-THYME AÏOLI VARIATION: Instead of mint, use 2 tablespoons lemon thyme.

ROQUEFORT DRESSING

MAKES ABOUT ½ CUP

1 tablespoon white vinegar

1 teaspoon English mustard

1 teaspoon Worcestershire sauce

½ teaspoon cayenne pepper

½ teaspoon salt

3 tablespoons vegetable oil

4 ounces Roquefort cheese, crumbled

In a food processor, combine vinegar, mustard, Worcestershire sauce, cayenne pepper, and salt. While blending, slowly add the oil through the top of the processor. Once smooth, scrape dressing into a bowl and add Roquefort. Whisk until smooth with no lumps.

CREAMY ROSEMARY MUSTARD

MAKES 1 QUART

3 tablespoons yellow mustard seed

1 tablespoon brown mustard seed

5 teaspoons minced fresh rosemary, divided

⅓ cup water

⅓ cup apple cider vinegar

½ cup white wine

¼ cup shallots, finely chopped

2 garlic cloves

1 cup heavy cream

1 tablespoon seedless Dijon mustard

1 cup mayonnaise (see page 230 or it better be Duke's)

Salt and pepper

Stir together the mustard seeds, 3 teaspoons minced rosemary, water, and vinegar in a bowl until all of the seeds are submerged. Cover and let sit at room temperature for three days.

In a saucepan, add the wine, shallots, and garlic. Bring to a boil and let simmer until reduced by half, about 10 minutes. Add cream and simmer until thick, about 12 to 15 minutes. Drain the mustard seeds and rosemary from the bowl and add those to the saucepan, along with the Dijon and the remaining 2 teaspoons of rosemary. Simmer for 2 more minutes. Remove from stove and let mixture come to room temperature. Pour mixture into a food processor. Add mayonnaise and blend until incorporated. Season with salt and pepper to taste.

GARLIC-HONEY AÏOLI

MAKES 2 ½ CUPS

2 cups mayonnaise (see page 230 or it better be Duke's)

6 garlic cloves, minced

½ teaspoon salt

½ teaspoon white pepper

2 teaspoons Maggi seasoning

¼ cup honey (I like to use a locally sourced sourwood honey)

In a food processor, blend together all ingredients except for the honey. Scrape the bottom and sides of the bowl, then add the honey and blend until evenly incorporated. It should be smooth and creamy.

LEMON-LOVAGE TARTAR SAUCE

MAKES 2 ½ CUPS

1 cup water

⅓ cup flour

2 egg yolks

1 cup vegetable oil

1 teaspoon salt

1 teaspoon white pepper

1 teaspoon garlic powder

2 tablespoons white wine vinegar

1 teaspoon coarse grain mustard

2 tablespoons fresh lemon juice

2 teaspoons lemon zest

½ cup fresh lovage, chopped fine

2 tablespoons fresh dill, chopped fine

¼ cup capers

¼ cup white onion, diced (optional)

Heat the water and flour in a saucepan over medium heat, stirring until a paste forms. Remove pan from heat and whisk egg yolks into mixture. Gradually add oil, whisking constantly. Transfer the mixture to a food processor and add the salt, white pepper, garlic powder, vinegar, mustard, lemon juice, and zest, then blend well until smooth. Add the lovage and dill, pulsing until evenly incorporated. (It may be necessary to scrape the bottom and sides of the processor if the herbs stick between pulses.) Transfer to a bowl and fold in the capers and onion. Chill before serving.

Lemon-Lovage Tartar Sauce pictured on page 135.

SORGHUM BBQ SAUCE

MAKES 1 ½ QUARTS

1 quart apple cider vinegar

8 tablespoons A-1 sauce

8 tablespoons Worcestershire sauce

¼ cup sorghum

1 ¼ sticks (10 ½ tablespoons) butter

3 tablespoons ketchup

3 teaspoons crushed red pepper

Salt and pepper to taste

1 ½ cups brown sugar (if making sweet barbecue sauce)

Combine ingredients in a saucepan. Simmer over medium-low heat, whisking occasionally until smooth and just starting to boil. If making sweet barbecue sauce, add 1½ cups brown sugar.

WOO GIRL RANCH

MAKES 1 QUART

4 garlic cloves

2 ½ cups mayonnaise (see page 230 or it better be Duke's)

½ cup sour cream

½ cup buttermilk

1 teaspoon salt

½ teaspoon black pepper

2 tablespoons fresh dill, finely chopped

In a food processor, combine the garlic and mayonnaise and blend until the garlic is completely incorporated and smooth. (It may be necessary to scrape the sides of the bowl with a rubber spatula a few times.) Add sour cream, buttermilk, salt, and pepper, pulsing until mixture is smooth. Transfer mixture to a bowl. Fold in chopped dill and store covered in a refrigerator until ready to serve.

BROWN GRAVY

MAKES 24 SERVINGS

THIS GRAVY CAN BE USED AS A FOUNDATION for fancy sauces by adding red wine, sherry, or madeira. It can also go right on top of your twice-baked or mashed potatoes.

1 pound veal bones	2 garlic cloves
1 carrot	6 tablespoons butter
1 yellow onion	2 quarts water
Pinch of thyme	Cornstarch
1 bay leaf	

Preheat oven to 400 degrees. Cut veal bones into pieces (a butcher can do this for you). Set bones in a roasting pan and cook until browned, about 20 to 30 minutes. Transfer bones to a large stock pot, along with carrot, onion, thyme, bay leaf, garlic, and butter. Add water and simmer over medium heat for 4 hours. Strain and discard solids. Thicken the liquid with cornstarch to desired consistency.

CRANBERRY SAUCE

MAKES 1 QUART

¼ cup freshly squeezed orange juice	3 apples, unpeeled, quartered, seeds removed
¼ teaspoon cinnamon	3 oranges, unpeeled, quartered, seeds removed
1 cup sugar	1 pound cranberries

Boil the orange juice, cinnamon, and ¼ cup of the sugar until reduced. Remove from heat and let cool. In a food processor, pulse together apples, oranges, and cranberries until all are evenly shredded but not mushy. Scrape sides and bottom of bowl a couple of times to ensure an evenly ground mixture. Transfer fruit to a bowl and fold in the remaining sugar and cooled orange juice reduction. Let stand covered in the refrigerator until ready to serve, preferably overnight. Will keep, covered, one week.

CORN VINEGAR

MAKES 1 GALLON

THIS IS AN EXCELLENT VINEGAR. We use our own filtered spring water at Hachland Hill to make it.

1 gallon rainwater, filtered

1 pint shelled Indian corn

½ pound sugar

Additional water as needed

In a stockpot, combine half of the filtered water and corn and bring to a boil, cooking until kernels burst. Transfer to a 2-gallon stone jug and add enough filtered rainwater to fill the jug halfway (replacing what evaporated from boiling). Dissolve the sugar in one cup of water by bringing to a boil. Pour into jug and stir or shake well. Cover the mouth of the jug with 2- to 3-inch thickness of cheese cloth. Let stand in a warm place, 75 to 80 degrees, for 1 month. Pour the vinegar into another jug, leaving half of the mother and repeat the process, adding more filtered water and sugar water to the original jug. To preserve this vinegar, cover the mouth of the jug with a piece of cloth and store in a dry warm place.

CHANTILLY CREAM

MAKES 1 QUART

2 cups heavy cream

1 tablespoon sugar

¼ teaspoon pure vanilla extract

In a stand mixer fitted with a whisk attachment, whip the cream for 2 minutes at medium speed. Add the sugar and vanilla, increase the speed to high, and continue to whip for about 6 minutes or until soft peaks form. Cover and refrigerate.

VANILLA-COFFEE SAUCE

MAKES 2 CUPS

1 cup light cream

¼ cup sugar

1 tablespoon pure vanilla extract

¼ cup strong coffee

1 tablespoon cornstarch

¼ cup cold water

Combine the cream, sugar, vanilla, and coffee in a saucepan over medium heat, stirring occasionally, until boiling. Dissolve cornstarch in water, then whisk cornstarch into sauce. Cook just until thick, being careful to not overcook.

SWISS MERINGUE BUTTERCREAM FROSTING

MAKES 1 QUART

165 grams (¾ cup) pasteurized egg whites

285 grams (scant 2 cups) sugar

450 grams (1 ¾ cups plus 1 tablespoon) unsalted butter

Pinch of salt (optional)

1 tablespoon preferred flavoring (an extract or a spice, optional)

In the bowl of a stand mixer fitted with a whisk attachment, lightly whisk together the egg whites and sugar. Place the bowl over a pot of simmering water, but do not let it touch the water. Lightly whisk the mixture by hand over the simmering water until it is just hot to the touch. Return the bowl to the stand mixer with the whisk attachment and whip on high speed until mixture doubles in volume. Continue to whip until meringue reaches stiff peaks and has completely cooled. Replace the whisk with a paddle attachment. While the mixer is running on low speed, add the butter a few pieces at a time until it is all incorporated. Add a pinch of salt or a tablespoon of your desired flavoring, if using. Increase the speed of the mixer and beat until the buttercream is light and fluffy.

ITALIAN BAKERS ICING

MAKES 1 QUART

THIS RECIPE MAKES A SOFT ICING—the more you beat it, the nicer the icing. If you desire to have your icing crust over, whisk the powdered sugar into the mixture just before spreading it on cake.

4 heaping tablespoons all-purpose flour

1 cup whole milk

¾ cup shortening

¾ cup sugar

1 teaspoon preferred flavoring

1 ½ cups powdered sugar (optional)

Whisk together flour and milk, then cook in a saucepan over low heat until it forms a ball of dough. Let the ball cool. Once cool, place dough in the bowl of a stand mixer fitted with a paddle attachment and beat until fluffy. Add the sugar and shortening to the dough mixture, beating after each addition. Continue beating until tripled in bulk. Add flavoring. If using, whisk in the powdered sugar just before spreading.

SEA FOAM

MAKES 24 SERVINGS

2 cups brown sugar

½ cup water

1 egg white

½ cup chopped nuts

1 teaspoon pure vanilla extract

Boil the sugar and water together until a little dropped in cold water forms a soft ball. In a stand mixer fitted with a paddle attachment, beat the egg white until stiff. Pour the hot sugar mixture over the beaten white and continue beating while pouring. Add the nuts and extract, then beat vigorously until the candy stiffens. When nearly set, drop spoonfuls onto parchment paper. Once chilled, the sea foam will harden so that it can be easily taken from the paper and eaten.

CRÈME PÂTISSIÈRE

MAKES 1½ QUARTS

946 grams (1 quart) milk

1 vanilla bean, split and scraped

250 grams (1 cup) sugar

100 grams (¼ cup) whole eggs

80 grams (⅓ cup) egg yolks

100 grams (¼ cup) pastry cream powder (or substitute cornstarch)

2 shots peach whiskey (I like Birddog)

Lay a sheet or two of plastic wrap down in a half sheet pan to completely cover its surface. Combine the milk, vanilla bean, and half (125 grams) of the sugar in a medium saucepan over medium heat. Bring the mixture to a boil, stirring occasionally with a rubber spatula. In a separate bowl, whisk together the whole eggs, egg yolks, remaining sugar, and pastry cream powder. Whisk hard until the mixture is smooth with no lumps and turns a pale yellow. Whisking constantly, pour a third of the boiling milk into the egg mixture to temper it. Add the tempered egg mixture to the saucepan with the remaining milk and place over medium-high heat. Add the shots of whiskey one at a time, quickly stirring between each addition. (You can fold in any fruit, chocolate, or other ingredient in lieu of the whiskey at this point to create your own flavor.) Boil for two minutes, stirring constantly to avoid burning the bottom, until it is fully cooked and has thickened to your desired consistency.

Remove the crème pâtissière from the heat and transfer it to the plastic wrap-covered sheet pan. Remove the vanilla bean and discard. Gently smooth out the mixture with a rubber spatula, then pull the edges of the plastic wrap together tightly over the crème, with the pieces overlapping to prevent a skin from forming on top. Invert the wrapped product and set aside to cool completely. Once it has cooled to room temperature, refrigerate the crème pâtissière until ready to use.

MARZIPAN

SERVES 12

1 egg white

1 cup almond paste

3 cups confectioners sugar

Lemon juice as needed

Glaze (recipe follows)

In a stand mixer fitted with a whisk attachment, beat egg white until fluffy. Switch whisk to a paddle attachment. Gradually work in almond paste. Add confectioners sugar and remove dough from bowl. Knead dough until it forms a paste that is easy to handle. If paste becomes too stiff, add lemon juice drop by drop. If it becomes too moist, add more sugar. Form into long rolls. Color and shape rolls to your preference. Attach garnishes if desired and let dry for 2 to 3 hours before applying glaze.

MARZIPAN GLAZE

½ cup sugar

¾ cup water

½ cup light corn syrup

Combine all ingredients in a saucepan and bring to a good boil. Boil for about 2 minutes or until it reaches 220 degrees on a candy thermometer. While still hot, apply to the marzipan candies using small paint brush. Let dry completely.

WATERMELON RIND PICKLES

SERVES 10

TRY THESE PICKLES with a mozzarella pearl and fresh mint leaf on a hot day!

1 large watermelon

2 tablespoons kosher salt

½ cup fresh lime juice

½ cup cane syrup

2 tablespoons sugar

½ cup rice wine vinegar

½ cup apple cider vinegar

1 kaffir lime leaf

1 tablespoon lemon verbena leaves

1 star anise pod

2 habanero peppers, halved

2 teaspoons candied ginger, minced

1 teaspoon allspice berries

1 teaspoon red pepper flakes

Break down the watermelon by slicing it into manageable pieces. Remove and discard the exterior green portion of the watermelon with a sharp peeler so that your rind is mostly white with a little pink on one side. Cut into 1-inch cubes. Juice enough of the melon's flesh to yield three cups of juice and reserve it for your pickling liquid.

Toss the rind cubes in the salt in a large bowl and let it rest until they have barely softened and taken the salt, about two hours.

Rinse the salted cubes in cold water and drain, then return them to the bowl. Add the watermelon and lime juice, syrup, sugar, vinegars, kaffir lime and lemon verbena leaves, star anise, habaneros, ginger, all spice berries, and red pepper flakes to stock pot, and bring to a boil. Stir while it is coming to a boil so that the syrup and sugar is totally incorporated into the liquid.

Strain the liquid into a pitcher and try to save the habaneros, lime and lemon verbena leaves, red pepper flakes, and star anise. Place the rind cubes in separate mason jars or a two-quart sealable jar/container and layer with the reserved spices above, then pour the liquid over top. Cover the jars and let them cool completely, then store in the refrigerator for at least 48 hours, until ready to eat.

CROCK JUG PICKLE RELISH

MAKES 24 SERVINGS

THIS RELISH goes great on a good bratwurst.

1 gallon vinegar

1 pound brown sugar

1 cup salt

2 ounces ground ginger

2 ounces ground mustard

1 ounce ground turmeric

1 cup grated horseradish

2 ounces black pepper

2 ounces white mustard seed

2 ounces celery seed

2 ounces whole cloves

Fresh chopped mixed vegetables (onions, cucumber, celery, cabbage, green tomatoes, red and green peppers, beans, carrots, corn, etc.)

Put vinegar in a 2-gallon crock jar. Add sugar, salt, and spices. Add fresh chopped mixed vegetables until crock is almost full. Be sure vinegar mixture covers the vegetables well. Weigh down with a plate or pan, and let it stand for two weeks before using.

DAMSON PRESERVES

MAKES 24 SERVINGS

THIS SUBSPECIES OF THE PLUM TREE is most commonly used in Great Britain. Tasting them in their raw state is sure to make you pucker, but they make divine preserves and jams. Its name is derived from the Latin (prunum) damascenum, meaning "plum of Damascus." Popular belief states that they were first cultivated in close proximity to the city of Damascus, the capital of modern-day Syria, and subsequently introduced to England by the Romans. Damson stones have occasionally been discovered in archaeological digs of ancient Roman camps across England. Today, they can be foraged in parks and woodlands throughout Great Britain, and you may be able to source them at fruit concentrated nurseries and orchards in the United States (they can be acquired online). This concentrated and luxurious flavor makes a wonderful addition to toast.

7 pounds damson plums

5 pounds sugar

2 oranges, ground whole

1 pound seeded raisins

5 cups water

Remove stones from damsons. Mix all ingredients in a large pot. Cook over medium-low heat for approximately 1 hour or until mixture is thick. Process small jars in warm water. Ladle the preserves into the jars and seal tight.

FRUIT & NUT GRANOLA

MAKES 12 SERVINGS

THIS IS GREAT DRY, served with milk, or over yogurt.

½ cup unsalted butter

⅓ cup light brown sugar

⅓ cup plus 1 teaspoon honey (I use local sourwood honey from Strange Honey Farm)

¼ teaspoon ground cinnamon

1 ¼ teaspoons pure vanilla extract

¾ teaspoon salt

1 cup rolled oats

⅔ cup coconut, finely grated

½ cup raw cashews, chopped into small pieces

½ cup raw pecans, chopped into small pieces

½ cup raw almonds, sliced

½ cup raw pistachios

½ cup raw walnuts, chopped into small pieces

3 tablespoons dried cranberries

3 tablespoons dried black currants

3 tablespoons dried blueberries

3 tablespoons dried apricots, cut into small pieces

3 tablespoons dried figs, stemmed and cut into small pieces

3 tablespoons dried cherries

3 tablespoons dried apple rings, cut into small pieces

3 tablespoons dried peaches, cut into small pieces

Preheat oven to 275 degrees. Combine the butter, brown sugar, honey, cinnamon, vanilla, and salt in a medium saucepan and bring to a simmer, stirring until the brown sugar is dissolved. Let mixture cool slightly. Combine the oats, coconut, and nuts in a large bowl and add the brown sugar mixture. Fold with a rubber spatula until everything is thoroughly coated. Spread out onto a parchment-lined sheet tray and bake for about 1 hour until golden, shuffling the oats and nuts three times throughout the cooking process. Remove from oven and evenly disperse the dried fruits over top. Bake for an additional 5 to 10 minutes. Remove from oven and let cool to room temperature. Break up the cooled granola as desired.

CRACKERS

MAKES 12 SERVINGS

1 cup all-purpose flour

2 teaspoons unsalted butter

½ teaspoon salt

1 egg, beaten

¼ cup whole milk

Preheat oven to 350 degrees. Combine all ingredients. Roll thin and sprinkle with salt. Cut into desired shapes. Pierce surface of each cracker with a fork. Bake in oven until golden brown and crispy.

CHEESE BISCUITS

MAKES 12 SERVINGS

A CUTE TIN OF THESE ZIPPY TREATS makes a wonderful gift any time of the year and beats the heck out of mixed nuts when your family needs to snack on something at a holiday gathering in anticipation of the big meal.

1 stick (½ cup) butter

¼ pound sharp cheddar cheese

1 cup all-purpose flour

½ teaspoon red pepper or to taste

½ teaspoon salt

Preheat oven to 350 degrees. Soften butter and cheese to room temperature. Blend together. Add dry ingredients and work together. Roll to ¼ inch thickness. Cut with small biscuit cutter or desired shape cutter. Place biscuits on parchment-lined half sheet tray and bake until biscuits begin to brown.

POTPOURRI JAR

MAKES 8 JARS

4 quarts mixed blossoms (roses, pinks, lemon verbena, tuberoses, violets, etc.)

1 cup salt

2 ounces allspice berries, crushed

2 ounces cinnamon stick, crushed

1 ounce cloves, crushed

2 nutmegs, coarsely grated

2 ounces ginger root, sliced thin

2 ounces orris root, sliced thin

½ pound dried lavender flowers

2 ounces dried orange peel, grated

2 ounces dried lemon peel, grated

½ ounce dried rosemary

1 pint cologne

Gather the blossoms early in the morning. Strip off the leaves and petals and spread on paper to dry in an attic or another airy, unused room. Once dry, measure out salt: For every 4 quarts of petals and leaves, use 1 cup of salt. In a large bowl, sprinkle ¼ cup of salt on the bottom then add 2 cups of petals, then more salt and more petals until all are used having salt for the top layer. Cover for 5 days, stirring twice daily. When moist, add the crushed allspice berries and cinnamon stick. Let this stand covered one week, turning daily. In a bowl, combine the remaining ingredients except for the cologne and mix well. Pack the petal mixture alternately with the spice mixture into jars. When filled, evenly distribute the cologne amongst the jars by pouring it over the top. Cover tight. Shake and stir every few days. Place potpourri jars in rooms. Lift off the top of the jars for a few minutes each day to keep your house smelling sweet.

DRYING FRUITS FOR WINTER

MAKES 1½ POUNDS

3 pounds fruit (I like to use
   apples, pears, and peaches)

6 tablespoons salt

1 cup sugar

1 gallon cold water

Peel fruits and cut into ¼-inch slices. Combine salt, sugar, and water, stirring until the salt and sugar have dissolved. Place sliced fruit in solution for several minutes. Spread out on platter or racks and dry in sun for 3 days, taking them in at night. Alternatively, dry them in an oven at 140 degrees for 6 to 24 hours, or until leathery. Store in a cool place in an airtight container.

INDEX

Note: Page numbers in *italics* indicate photographs.

MORE GREAT BOOKS *from*
BLUE HILLS PRESS

Little Everyday Cakes
$22.95 | 160 Pages

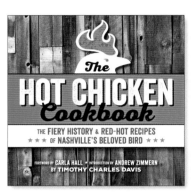

The Hot Chicken Cookbook
$22.95 | 128 Pages

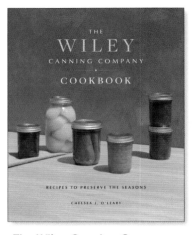

The Wiley Canning Company Cookbook
$35.00 | 248 Pages

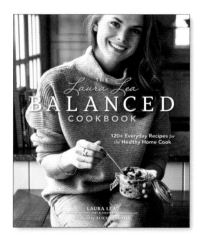

The Laura Lea Balanced Cookbook
$35.00 | 368 Pages

Simply Laura Lea
$35.00 | 368 Pages

BLUE HILLS
PRESS

Look for these Blue Hills Press titles at your favorite bookstore, specialty retailer, or visit *www.bluehillspress.com*.
For more information about Blue Hills Press, email us at *info@bluehillspress.com*.